THE $5 *Chef*

FAMILY COOKBOOK

FAMILY COOKBOOK

*Great-Tasting Meals
on a Budget!*

Marcie Rothman

PRIMA PUBLISHING

PRIMA PUBLISHING and colophon are registered trademarks of Prima Communications, Inc.
The $5 Chef and logo are trademarks of Marcie Rothman.

Library of Congress Cataloging-in-Publication Data

Rothman, Marcie.
The $5 chef family cookbook: great-tasting meals on a budget! /
Marcie Rothman.
p. cm.
Includes index.
ISBN 0-7615-0653-5
1. Low budget cookery. I. Title.
TX652.R676   1996
641.5'52—dc20   96-34588
                                                                        CIP
97 98 99 00 01 HH 10 9 8 7 6 5 4 3 2
Printed in the United States of America

HOW TO ORDER
Single copies may be ordered from Prima Publishing, P.O. Box 1260BK, Rocklin, CA 95677; telephone (916) 632-4400. Quantity discounts are also available. On your letterhead, include information concerning the intended use of the books and the number of books you wish to purchase.

Visit us online at http://www.primapublishing.com

To continued great meals and wonderful company with family and friends.

And to my dad who always said, "Taste it, you might like it."

The universe does not have laws.

It has habits.

And habits can be broken.

—Tom Robbins, *Jitterbug Perfume*

What's common sense

just isn't common practice.

—Stephen Covey, author of
The Seven Habits of Highly Effective People

Contents

Acknowledgments

My sincere thanks to everyone who helped make this book happen (appearing in alphabetical order):

Elaine Corn, friend and fellow cook

Suzanne Hertfelder, who loves good food—just doesn't cook

Dewey Hopper and my crew at KOVR-TV, my best testers

Dena Kaye, my best friend and always there

Brenda Nichols, my project editor with unsurpassed patience

Leo Pearlstein at Lee and Associates, who gave me my break for television years ago

Frank Pipgras, my sweetie, whose choices of wine blend well with my knowledge of food

Everyone at Prima Publishing for making this book happen

Rita Rothman, an editorial expert who knows good food

Shirley Rothman, my mom, who has an unsurpassed eye for detail

Jennifer Basye Sander, my editor, without whom this book would not be possible

Dawn Simms, childhood friend and cook, who helped sift through the recipes

Karen Stabiner, friend, cook, and writer

Tom Waters, computer wizard

Introduction

In a frazzle over what foods to eat? Confused by never-ending studies about fat, salt, and nutrition? Want food that is quick and convenient to prepare, low in cost, and tastes good, too? You are not alone—just look at Cathy in the cartoon.

As the $5 Chef on television, I have shown millions how to cook great food quickly and inexpensively, specifically, how to make delicious $5 meals that feed four. Economy is becoming more and more important—whether we are single, senior citizens, or families, we all want value when we shop. If you doubt that it is possible to eat well on a budget, then read on.

A steady diet of typically high-fat commercially made fast food may be dangerous to your budget and your health. A 1996 study by the Food Marketing Institute (FMI) shows that many of us are not eating the recommended five servings of vegetables and fruits each day because of the perceived inconvenience of storing and preparing them. As you will discover in this book, buying, storing, and preparing fresh foods is easier than you might think.

Just consider the money you will save: On the average, a pound of prepared potato salad serves four and costs about $2. Depending on store specials, $2 can buy ten pounds of potatoes (that's $0.20 a pound and a lot of potatoes). But that's just the beginning. At home, that sack of spuds makes many dishes from salads to sides and baked to boiled in just a few minutes, especially with the help of a microwave oven. That same sack of fresh potatoes offers far more variety and nourishment than the four servings of costly, commercially prepared potato salad you could have bought for the same amount of money.

This book will show you how to shop for great-tasting, inexpensive, wholesome food prepared quickly at home. You will find shopping tips that save money and time and cooking tips that make food fast and easy to prepare. You will even gain a new way of thinking about food.

CATHY by Cathy Guisewite

CATHY ©1995 Cathy Guisewite. Reprinted with permission of UNIVERSAL PRESS SYNDICATE. All rights reserved.

Variety is the spice of life, and a well-stocked cupboard places that variety at your fingertips. Think of your cupboard (and refrigerator) as a treasure trove of last-minute ingredients. You can create easy, fast food dishes with canned beans or dried pasta, or jazz up an old favorite with a splash of vinegar, a pinch of an herb, or a dab of mustard. This book includes a list of foods for a well-stocked cupboard and a chart that places herbs and spices into ethnic categories for easy reference.

Recipes are arranged alphabetically by main ingredient. That means if you want a potato recipe, you will find all potato recipes under "potatoes" rather than by the usual entrée or appetizer listing. Menu planning is simple because all the recipes are listed by category in the index.

The $5 Chef Family Cookbook: Great-Tasting Meals on a Budget! is packed with common sense, easy and universal tips, valuable information, and quick and nutritious recipes that work for today's busy families.

THE $5 *Chef*

FAMILY COOKBOOK

CHAPTER I

FOOD AWARENESS BEGINS AT HOME

My wise mother recently remarked that we learn to cook the food we grew up eating. How true that is, given the number of people who do not know, for example, that chickens are not born deep-fried and frozen, or that corn and peaches are not grown in cans.

My love affair with food began when I was knee-high to my mother. When she made homemade chocolate pudding, I was always there to lick the bowl. (That was before the days of pulling the top off an individual serving of premade pudding.) When Mom and I went shopping it was for fruits and vegetables growing in a certain season. Tomatoes, zucchini, watermelons, and peaches were summer foods, while apples, pears, oranges, bananas, and thick-skinned squash were winter staples. I learned to love food—real food—from my mother and her mother, my grandma Julia.

TO CHEW ON

Our food tells us where we came from and who we are.

What is real food? It's edibles in their raw and natural state cooked with a minimum of fuss and a maximum of flavor. When I am asked what I think of margarine, sugar substitutes, or artificial foods, I can only say that I grew up on real butter, real sugar, and real chocolate. While butter, sugar, and the like may translate to fat, calories, and extra pounds, I eat those foods in moderation and with an awareness of what and how much I am eating. The point is that a little of the real thing goes a long way. Moderation is my middle name. I want my calories to count, and I want to enjoy food with flavor, so I avoid products with artificial flavorings and ingredients I can't pronounce.

Living in Los Angeles in the sixties and seventies, I took many ethnic cooking classes and gave dinner parties exposing my friends to new and different foods. It seemed that almost everyone was on some kind of diet—a new one sprouted up practically monthly. Chinese food was always a favorite, and early on I began to play with the recipes. I would use less oil for the stir-fry, cut down on the deep-fried foods, and reduced the amount of soy sauce. I found it easier to put the bottle of soy on the table for each guest to add at will. My friends began to notice how good fresh ingredients tasted, rather than how they tasted masked with salt or fat.

Of the many students I've taught over the years, some couldn't cook, yet wanted to feed their family more than just processed foods. Take my friend Kate who never learned to cook very well because her mom did not cook very much . . . though she did make fabulous tacos. When Kate married and her husband had health problems, she learned that good food could be cooked quickly, from mostly fresh rather than processed and boxed ingredients. She became aware of food ingredient labels so she could decide how much salt she wanted.

Compared with today's standards, food labeling was just beginning in the sixties, seventies, and eighties. Then there were no listings or percentages for fat, sodium, calories, or portions—only ingredients. One learned quickly to spot the salt and other additives in processed foods.

Today, new diets continue to sprout almost monthly and the words really haven't changed—fat, salt, cholesterol, and fiber are the current buzz. My cooking continues to evolve and over the past few years I've increased my awareness of what and how I eat.

In a December, 1994, *Newsweek* article, Laura Shapiro wrote, "America is in the grip of a fat fanaticism, obsessed with the furtive grams of fat that lurk in our food plotting hostile takeovers of our health and our waistlines." According to a 1996 Food Marketing Institute (FMI) study done with *Prevention*, fat content is the first item shoppers look for on a label and concerns more than half of supermarket shoppers.

Despite our national obsession with fat, nearly 60 percent of Americans do not follow the United States Department of Agriculture's (USDA) Food Guide Pyramid, which recommends, among other things, a combined minimum of five servings a day of fruits and vegetables (known as Five-A-Day). A serving is ½ to 1 cup of fresh vegetables or fruit. The USDA guidelines also suggest we use fats, oils, and sweets sparingly and eat a variety of foods including more breads and grains.

Does it cost more in time and money to eat healthier? Not when we consider the cost of premade and packaged "convenience" foods that may take as long or longer to prepare than fresh foods. The 1996 FMI study offers some clues about why we haven't changed our eating habits. The study shows that we want our food to be fast and convenient, and that many people perceive that fresh fruits and vegetables are inconvenient because they are difficult to store and prepare.

It is possible to change our eating habits, and this book will help show you that doing so is neither expensive nor inconvenient. It's all a matter of tuning in to what you're spooning into your body.

We are what we eat. Awareness means taking note of how you feel when you eat greasy, salty, fatty, high-calorie foods. It's also all about making choices—no one said we can't eat those "bad" foods, but we do have a choice about how much and how often we do. Consider that much of how and what we eat is based on habit, and habits can be changed.

CHAPTER 2

TUNE IN TO WHAT YOU SPOON IN

Habits can be broken . . . and changed if you consider it a gradual process. You may not change the way you eat overnight, but you will eventually find yourself eating better and spending less. Here are some quick tips to start you on the way.

SOME QUICK TIPS

Cut Back, Not Out

- If fat- and sodium-laden fast foods are a daily habit, try a weekly indulgence instead. Or eat these foods less frequently and in smaller portions. Note the money you save.

- Eat less of something that's a habit. For example, instead of slathering butter on bread, try halving your usual amount. A little taste goes a long way.

- When it comes to sugar, chocolate, and butter, give me a little of the real thing because substitutes and artificial foods make my mouth feel funny. Try not to deny yourself that favorite (probably sinful) food. Take a smaller portion, have a few bites, and leave the rest, or share it with a pal.

Tune in to Fat and Calories

- Calories do count. If something is fat free, it may be filled with sugar or other sweeteners that add calories.

- Rather than being a mathematician and figuring out the percentage of fat in a day's worth of food, keep track by adding up the fat grams listed on product labels.

- Remember a tablespoon of fat, be it vegetable or olive oil, butter, or margarine, has 9 grams of fat. Period.

- Give yourself less to count: Eat more fresh foods, especially fruits and vegetables, which have virtually no fat unless it is added when making or serving a dish.

Savor the Flavor

- In his book, *Eat More, Weigh Less,* Dr. Dean Ornish explains a method for eating. He writes about "meditating" on a bite of whatever you love to eat. Notice I said a bite . . . of anything, high or low fat, sinful or healthy. Consider meditation as a way to *pay attention* to what you eat. The first few bites usually taste the best. It's easy to overeat when we forget to *notice* what the food tastes like. Try this trick and you can still eat your favorite foods in moderation.

- Savor the meal as well as the food. We've become so mobile that for many (including myself), eating in the car is a foregone conclusion. It's also very unsafe. In this crazy, fast-moving world we live in, try to make some quiet time to eat, relax, and enjoy the company of family or friends.

TEACH YOUR CHILDREN WELL

Food awareness begins at home. Debbie, a mom with three young children, told me how she taught her kids to notice when they have too much sugar. She gave them each a cookie and asked them to pay attention to how they felt. Her kids can tell her when they feel zingy after too much sugar.

Parents play a part in how kids eat. David Shaw writes in his book, *The Pleasure Police*, that anxiety about diet is everywhere: Even very young children are consumed about dieting for fear of getting fat.

Difficult as it may be, try to keep your food fears (getting too fat) or dislikes (of certain foods) to yourself. Sharing negative comments with kids can reinforce a dislike of a food and create bad eating habits. A case in point: Recently while I was teaching a cooking class for women and children, the subject was fresh carrots. One mother said she didn't like most vegetables, including carrots. After the class, her child came up and asked for a carrot. As he began to eat it, his mother asked why he had taken the carrot when he "knew he didn't like carrots." He then stopped eating and gave up the carrot. Without his mom's negative spin, perhaps this child would have found the carrot to his liking.

Let kids decide after they've tasted something whether they want it again. Try to take a positive attitude about food. Explain moderation, variety, balance, and enjoyment of all foods.

Get the kids in the habit of helping in the kitchen. Encourage them to try a new food, or help you mix a dressing, prepare food for cooking, even set the table. Make it "cool" to eat healthy foods.

TO CHEW ON

Good eating habits begin at home.

PORTIONS

Many of us think that bigger is better—even when it comes to food. Volume is perceived as value and large portion sizes indulge that thought. In March 1996, *The Wall Street Journal* noted that when visitors from other countries eat in American restaurants, they are shocked by the huge portions of food. The article compares two pizza restaurants— one in London, England, the other on Long Island, New York. Portions at the slightly upscale London eatery consist of 9 ounces for pasta and 8 ounces for meat or fish. Meanwhile in New York, value-hungry patrons get 16 ounces of pasta, nearly 16 ounces of fish, and almost 24 ounces of meat. More isn't always better, especially when consumed at one meal.

At home, moderate portions are as good for your health as your pocketbook. Consider the money saved when portions are moderately trimmed. Generally portions sizes are: ½ to 1 cup for fruits and vegetables. A serving of meat, fish or poultry is 3 to 6 ounces or a piece that fits in the palm of your hand. Take a culinary and cultural hint from Asian cuisine and use meats, poultry, and fish as accents or side dishes. Create volume with fruits, vegetables, grains, pasta, and other such foods. We can still eat all our favorite dishes if we tune in to moderation and enjoy a variety of foods.

TO CHEW ON

A pint is a pound the world around—16 ounces = 1 pound.

If you want to eat less candy, look for the individually wrapped bite-size pieces that cost $0.05 or $0.10 each. Then you can have a bit of something sweet without blowing it. You will save money, too, if you have one piece of candy ($0.10) instead of a whole candy bar ($0.50).

CHAPTER 3

MARKETING AWARENESS

BEFORE YOU SHOP: TUNE IN TO THESE MONEY-SAVING TIPS

- Consider your lifestyle and food needs: Do you eat in the car or at the kitchen sink? Does the kitchen look like a restaurant where everyone cooks and eats something different at the same meal? Are there special dietary needs such as reducing fat, cholesterol, salt, and sugar? Your lifestyle plays a part in the foods you buy.

- Your lifestyle helps to determine your cooking style: How much time do you have to prepare a meal? If you're always on the go, think salads, fruits, and vegetables that combine into simple, yet elegant meals. If you like to spend time cooking over the weekend, experiment with new recipes and cook make-ahead casseroles, soups, and stews for the next week.

- Plan roughly a week's worth of meals at a time: What does your schedule look like for the coming week? You'll save time shopping and spend less if you know when you won't be cooking at home. Less food will wither in the refrigerator if you only buy what you need for the week.

- Check your cupboard, refrigerator, and freezer to replenish staples (pasta, rice, sauces, salsas, peanut butter, tuna, eggs, milk, frozen vegetables, and other necessities).

- Read newspaper food ads for store specials on produce, poultry, fish, meat, and staples.

- Plan menus with lots of fresh produce and some meat and dairy. Fresh food usually costs less than such budget busters as prepackaged, boxed, frozen, or carryout foods. Aside from carryout foods, which can be expensive, many convenience foods may not be as quick to make as their fresh counterparts.

- Include planned-overs (fresh or frozen foods used for more than one meal) in your menus. Planned-overs take advantage of store specials such as a large cut of meat, a ten-pound sack of potatoes, or three heads of lettuce.

- Check the refrigerator for leftovers and incorporate them in your meal plan. For example: Toss leftover chicken or meat into a salad or top leftover vegetables with your favorite dressing.

- Shop smart with a shopping list. Spend a few moments to make a list or add to an ongoing one. The list keeps you focused, organized, and efficient while shopping. It helps move you faster through the store because it eliminates the temptation to cruise the aisles for costly impulse items. A list also helps you avoid duplicating items already on hand and overbuying fresh produce that may spoil and go to waste.

- Coupons, at least the variety that are slipped into Sunday newspapers, have become shopping dinosaurs. Fewer than 2 percent of 291.9 billion coupons distributed in 1995 were redeemed. Traditionally coupons save money on favorite brands, however, they also encourage brand switching. And they are rarely offered for fresh produce or meats. Look for in-store coupons near a particular product, or on the Internet (California is the test market). Check weekly market specials for as good or better buys. Also consider generic brands for price and quality.

- Where you shop can make a difference in your food bill. Avoid expensive convenience stores for everyday shopping. Shop warehouse stores for large quantity food bargains. (Note: you may need a warehouse at home to store the large packages.) Avoid the "supermarket hop" (shopping many markets for a bargain here and a bargain there). Hopping from one place to the next wastes time and money in the market and increases transportation costs as well.

AT THE MARKET SHOPPING TIPS

- Remember to take along your shopping list. It saves time and money and keeps you focused on shopping.

- Notice the layout of the supermarket and the location of the bakery (including coffee bars) and prepared deli foods. Many times these kiosks are stationed near the store entrance to promote noshing while shopping. While prepared foods may be convenient, if you want to save cash, don't make them a daily habit.

TO CHEW ON

Get a few neighbors or family members together to buy foods in bulk and share the savings. A variation: Combine shopping lists, check supermarket ads, and shop different supermarkets for best buys. Share the savings in time and money.

- Notice where the fresh produce, meat, and dairy sections are—usually around the walls of the market. Shop these areas first, then the inner aisles. The inner aisles carry canned and bottled foods along with many budget busters, those high-priced packaged convenience and frozen foods.

- It's no bargain to buy meat, produce, or dairy that isn't fresh. Be flexible and make ingredient substitutions at the market to avoid high prices, food past its prime, or unavailability of a product.

- Shopping with the kids or on an empty stomach increases the chances that your cart will fill with snacks, candy, chips, and other processed foods.

- Buy rice, pastas, grains, dried beans, candies, and cookies in the bulk food section. Bulk foods allow you to buy as much or as little as you need, and prices are generally lower than similar prepackaged foods.

- Look for unit pricing labels on the shelf near each product in the market. These labels show the cost per ounce, pound, pint, or other measure for the food product. Read labels, compare prices of different brands and sizes of the same item. Don't forget to check generic brands. Use unit pricing to compare the cost of prepackaged and convenience foods versus the fresh equivalent.

- End-of-the-aisle displays may not always be cheaper. Be sure to compare other sizes of the competitive products.

- Note sell or pull-by date or best-if-eaten-by labels on meat and dairy products. This is the date the store must remove or sell the item. Look for bargains on day-old produce (usually packaged separately and placed on a rack in the produce section). Good buys can be found on dairy and meat that are near the sell or pull-by date. Look for steaks and roasts. *Buy any of these items only if they will be used within a day or two of purchase.* Otherwise it could mean throwing food and money down the drain.

Prepackaged Versus Raw Foods

Product	Quantity	Total
Prepackaged herbed rice	7.2 ounces serves 7	$1.25
Raw rice	2 pounds serves 32	$1.35
Frozen chicken dinner	Serves 1	$3.00
Raw chicken	3 pounds serves 4	$3.50
Bottle salad dressing	16 ounces (1 pint)	$3.00
Homemade dressing	16 ounces (1 pint)	$1.00

Approximate prices, depending on specials, location, availability

■ Read labels carefully for ingredients and nutrients. Ingredients are listed with the most first and least last. Check for cooking instructions and time. Many times what we think is convenient and fast in the form of processed food is neither. While frozen dinners may need 15 or 20 minutes in the oven, a cut-up chicken can be broiled in the same or less time. Boxed, seasoned convenience rice takes the same 20 minutes to cook as raw bagged rice, and raw is cheaper and more versatile.

Food for Thought

■ Homemade dressings are a cinch to make—most of the ingredients are probably already on hand in the refrigerator or cupboard. Bottled dressings may be convenient, but there's a price (about $3 for one pint or two cups) and those dressings may contain lots of fat, sodium, and preservatives. For comparison, a quart (four cups) of low-fat mayonnaise is about $2.85.

■ For a fast side dish or salad that's a good source of dietary fiber, low in fat, and best of all, inexpensive, look no further than the bean (legume) section of the supermarket. Save time and buy them canned ($0.59 to $0.99 for 15 ounces— about 2 cups, depending on the type of bean). Save money and buy them dry to cook yourself (roughly the same price as canned for a pound, which makes about 5 cups cooked).

■ Avoid the following foods whenever possible. They may increase sugar, salt, and fat in a meal. They will also put a dent in your budget.

Out of season fresh fruits and vegetables

Sauced and seasoned frozen vegetables

Sugarcoated cereals

High-fat packaged cookies, cakes, pies, and buns

High-fat chips, dips, and puffs

Frozen prepared meals

Soft drinks

Candy

High-fat dairy products

■ Try these foods instead:

Fresh fruits and vegetables, in season

Unadorned frozen fruits and vegetables such as peaches, berries, corn, green beans, and peas

Cereals sweetened with juice concentrate

Pretzels, graham crackers, and other nonfried snacks

Raisins and other dried fruit

Lowfat dairy products including cheese, milk, ice cream, and sour cream

Jellies and jams sweetened with fruit concentrates

Produce

Shop Seasonally Different crops grow best in summer, fall, winter, or spring, and come to market at their prime during that particular season. Prices are lower for produce that is in the peak of its growing season. For example, tomatoes in winter are colorless, flavorless, and expensive. During the summer months, local tomatoes are brilliant red, juicy, flavorful, and cheap. Eating foods seasonally naturally helps us pay attention to our body's food needs—we eat heavier meals when it's cold and lighter ones when it's warm.

Weather is always a factor in the price of foods. Within particular seasons, some produce has a short window of peak availability; look for specials on such produce as strawberries, apricots, or asparagus.

Prewashed and cut lettuce and vegetables are convenient. Note the cost per pound and try to buy these when they are on special.

Rule of thumb: A pound of fruit or vegetables feeds three to four.

- Buy produce in season.

- Spend about $0.69 a pound for produce in season or on special.

- Read the supermarket ads and once in the market look for produce on special

- Check for day-old produce packaged separately, usually at a lower cost. Depending on freshness and quality, it's a good buy for higher priced produce.

- Include in menus fresh mushrooms, snow peas, and other year-round, high-priced vegetables and fruits. A few of them sliced or slivered go a long way.

Poultry

Rule of thumb: A whole fryer, 3 to 3½ pounds, feeds 4. Cooked and shredded, the meat goes a long way when added to lettuce, vegetables, beans, rice, or other foods.

- Watch for store specials on whole fryers or parts.

- Compare a whole chicken at roughly $0.59 to $0.99 a pound to a pound of breasts at $3.75 or more a pound. A whole chicken makes many meals: Use back and neck for soup stock, breasts for stir-fry, legs and thighs for salads.

- Use whole turkeys and parts now available year-round.

- Most ground turkey is low in fat and easily substitutes for other ground meats. Do read package labels for fat content.

Meat

Rule of thumb: A pound serves three to four people about four ounces each, depending on fat and water content. Look

TO CHEW ON

Hints for cutting up a whole bird: With bird on its back, gently pull wings and thighs/legs away from body and cut skin to expose joints. Cut wings first, at joint attached to body. Then cut thighs/legs. Cut between rib joints to separate back from breast. To split breast, lay skin-side down and make a small cut at top of breast in white cartilage near wishbone. Remove brown bone (keel) from the meat.

for percentage of fat per pound in ground meat. Low-priced ground beef may be high in fat, so it's not always a wise buy.

- Take a hint from Asian cuisine: Use meat as a side dish, rather than as a main course. A whole steak serves four if thinly sliced after cooking and served with healthier main attractions of vegetables, pastas, rice, or beans.

- Watch for specials. Buy larger cuts of beef, lamb, or pork to freeze for later meals if you can use the quantity. Store specials allow for good steaks or roasts when the price is right.

- If time is short, look for cut-up and ready-to-cook marinated meats that take less preparation time. Note, they may cost more than meat cut or marinated at home.

- If time is available, consider buying a large cut of meat such as chuck roast to process at home into hamburger and other dishes.

Seafood

Rule of thumb: A pound serves 4 roughly 4 ounces each.

- Fish is a good source of protein that cooks quickly.

- Look for specials on high-ticket seafood such as shrimp. Buy a few and cut them in pieces to stretch the quantity.

- Fish that smells fishy or like ammonia, is not fresh.

- "Fresh frozen" means that fish or seafood has been frozen when caught and then sold thawed. It should be labeled "previously frozen." Fresh frozen or frozen may cost less than fresh.

- Fresh whole fish have clear, full eyes; bright red or pink gills; moist shiny skin; and firm, elastic flesh that bounces back to the touch.

- Soft, mushy flesh may be a sign of age or refrozen thawed fish.

Breads

- Look for day-old breads and bakery products at the supermarket or bakery outlet stores. Use it to make homemade croutons and bread crumbs.

TO CHEW ON

We never repent of having eaten too little.

—Thomas Jefferson

CHAPTER 4

HERBS AND SPICES

Herbs and spices are a cook's best friend. A pinch of cumin, cinnamon, or basil can add a new dimension to the same old boring dish. Have a varied stash of dried herbs and spices on hand to give pizzazz to your cooking.

Spicing Hints

- New to herbs and spices? Pick one or two flavors, use a pinch in the recipe, and then taste and add more if desired.

- When cooking, always taste the food to adjust the seasoning for your palate.

- Add more spice or another flavor if the food seems too bland.

- Too many flavors overpower the subtle taste of good fresh ingredients. Refer to the spice chart (page 266–267) to choose flavors that work well together.

- Try garlic: Used in nearly every cuisine, it enhances the flavor of a variety of dishes, and works well with herbs and spices. Use fresh garlic whenever possible.

- Look for fresh herbs in the produce section or grow your own.

- To store fresh herbs, rinse and dry them first. Refrigerate in plastic, or with stems in water, covered with a plastic bag.

- To increase the flavor of dried herbs, crush them in your fingers, then add to food.

- If you want to cut back on salt, try herbs and spices to punch up flavors. Check the spice chart (page 266–267) for ideas.

- When possible, buy herbs and spices in bulk rather than in the small bottles. Since you don't pay for packaging, bulk prices may be less than the jars of herbs and you can buy as much as you need.

- Store dried herbs and spices away from heat and light.

Herb Mixtures

Go international by trying new spices and blends available in the spice section of the supermarket: Use a sparing pinch or two to zip up rice, salads, dressings, dips, or vegetables.

Fine herbs: For French and Italian dishes, this is a mixture of tarragon, parsley, chives, and other specified fresh or dried herbs.

Five-spice powder: For an Asian twist, this is a mixture of star anise, fennel (both slightly licorice tasting), Szechwan peppercorns, cloves, and cinnamon.

Garam masala: For an Indian flavor, this is usually cardamom, black pepper, cumin, coriander, cinnamon, and cloves.

Curry powder: A blend of many spices, made yellow by turmeric.

There are numerous other blends on the market, including poultry, grilling, Thai, Mexican, baking, and vegetable. Many are salt free and very good.

Beyond Herbs and Spices

Bring up the flavors in a dish with a squeeze of lemon juice or a dash of orange or lemon zest (grated outer peel); a drop or two of vinegar, Tabasco, or Worcestershire sauce; or a pinch of cayenne or freshly ground pepper or salt.

CHAPTER 5

IN THE CUPBOARD

STAPLES

Fast food sometimes means using foods that are already on hand in the cupboard or refrigerator. This is a sampling of foods—add your favorites.

Fresh

Onions, garlic, ginger, and parsley:

- A head of garlic consists of many cloves (not the tiny black pungent spice used on ham). Buy white or purple heads that have no soft or black spots. When it comes to garlic, convenience does come in a jar: you can buy garlic puréed or chopped. Be sure to read the label for oil and/or preservatives. Fresh garlic keeps well in a cool dry place with good ventilation. Avoid plastic bags—they create

TO CHEW ON

Garlic is as good as ten mothers.
—Les Blank

moisture that rots garlic. To peel a clove, loosen skin by smashing with the flat side of a knife.

- Fresh garlic, onion, ginger, parsley, and cilantro have better flavor than their dried counterparts. Check bottles of dried herbs for fresh/dried equivalents. For a rough rule of thumb, figure ½ teaspoon any herb equals 1 tablespoon fresh.

- Buy onions that are firm to the touch with no soft spots. As with garlic, keep in a cool dry place with good ventilation and avoid plastic bags. Do keep a bottle of dried chopped onions to use when onions aren't good or you need a last-minute burst of flavor for a dish.

- When possible use fresh parsley. Sprigs add color and texture as a garnish. Wash and dry the parsley and refrigerate in a plastic bag.

- Chew a sprig or two of fresh parsley for a nice tasting mouth.

- A little fresh ginger goes a long way. Chopped, grated, or sliced, its pungent flavor zips up stir-fries, salad dressings, and marinades.

- Store ginger refrigerated in a covered jar filled with white wine or sherry, or freeze for up to a month wrapped in plastic. I prefer to use it unpeeled—its essence is just below the skin. Use crystallized, preserved, or pickled ginger in some Asian dishes or for baking.

Lemons, oranges, limes: When in season and good buys, keep fresh citrus on hand. The juice or zest (the finely grated peel) gives a gentle flavor boost to just about any dish.

Eggs: Whites are protein, yolks are fat and cholesterol, use them sparingly.

Dairy

Milk, cheese, sour cream, yogurt, butter, or margarine: The low- and nonfat versions of many of these products work just fine most of the time. A word about cheese: I prefer to cut the amount of cheese in a recipe, especially those that use shredded cheese, rather than use nonfat cheese that, to me, tastes like flavored glue.

Dry

Pasta, noodles, rice, beans, lentils, dried peas, couscous, and bulgur: Buy these dry goods in their raw state, not pre-seasoned and packaged. They keep almost indefinitely and, aside from the beans, can be cooked in 20 minutes or less. All are practically fat free in their raw state and only become fatty when oil, butter, margarine, or cheese are added. Asian rice and cellophane (bean thread) noodles also store well for quick use in soups and salads. Couscous and bulgur need no cooking and fluff up in just minutes with the addition of hot liquid.

Flour (I use unbleached, all-purpose), sugar, salt, chocolate chips, unsweetened cocoa, baking powder, and baking soda: These are a must for cakes, muffins, cookies, and other baked goods.

Flavored extracts: Vanilla-, almond-, and lemon-flavored extracts are a must for baking. Try to use real rather than imitation flavors. Use sparingly as the flavor is very concentrated and a small bottle seemingly lasts forever!

Dried fruits: Raisins, in particular, make easy snacks and add texture and color to salads, curries, cookies, and more.

Nuts and seeds: Unsalted and unroasted almonds, peanuts, walnuts, sesame, or your favorites are great for cooking or snacking. Nuts are high in fat so use them with caution.

Many times I use a sprinkling of sesame seeds or chipped walnuts or almonds as a crunchy garnish for salads, vegetables, or baked goods. Look for nuts in the bulk food section—this way you buy what you need and avoid the temptation to "have just one more."

Canned/Bottled

Tomato products: Tomato sauce, tomato paste, and ketchup.

Canned beans: Keep some of all types including garbanzos, kidney, pinto, black, and white. Most are high in fiber and low in fat and make fast salads, dips, or additions to other dishes.

Seafood: Tuna and anchovies.

Sauces: Barbecue, soy, hoisin (Chinese sweet and salty for poultry or vegetables), Worcestershire, Tabasco, and others.

Chicken and beef broth: Look for low-sodium varieties.

Condiments: Olives, pickles, salsas, chutneys, chili sauces, and pickles.

PB&J: Peanut butter, jellies, and jams (look for those made with all fruit and no added sugars).

Mustards: Varieties include ballpark, Dijon, honey, and dried. Mustard keeps well and always adds zip to a dish.

Oils: Vegetable oil, olive oil, Asian sesame oil (it is dark with a very intense flavor, use sparingly)

Nonstick sprays: Use instead of butter or oil to prevent sticking when baking or frying food.

Vinegars: Stock a range of varieties and flavors including: rice, wine, sherry, raspberry, balsamic, white, and cider. A little goes a long way to bring up flavors in a dish. Vinegars have a long shelf life.

Wine: Look for specials on varietals: Cabernet Sauvignon, Zinfandel, Sauvignon Blanc, Chenin Blanc, Chardonnay.

Juices: Tomato or V-8 (for entrées and sauces); apple and pineapple (for baking, poaching, or sauces); clam juice (for seafood sauces and dishes).

Marinated vegetables: Peppers and artichoke hearts

Frozen

Apple, orange, and other fruit juice concentrates

Bulk frozen vegetables and fruits: Unsauced and unseasoned peas, corn, green beans, or broccoli make colorful dishes or additions to salads, casseroles, and pasta. Berries and peaches packed without any sugar or syrup make easy last-minute desserts.

KITCHEN EQUIPMENT

Good food depends on good ingredients, not expensive cookware and gadgets. It is possible to cook well with a few good pots and utensils. A case in point is Chinese cooking: This cuisine uses spartan utensils—a wok, perhaps another pot, and a cleaver—to create quick, mouthwatering dishes from fresh ingredients.

How much equipment you have depends on your particular needs; these vary depending on how many you cook for, the size of your kitchen, and the storage space you have available. Do spend a little money for a few good knives, pots, pans, and a garlic press. Buy them in department stores, gourmet shops, or even hardware stores. Sometimes basic gadgets and pots and pans are cheaper in the supermarket, but beware of poor quality. If equipment falls apart six months after purchase, it isn't worth the so-called savings.

Knives: A sharp knife makes chopping and cutting a cinch. You will spend less time and energy chasing food around a cutting board if you use sharp knives. My three favorite knives are a good eight-inch chef's knife, a vegetable and fruit slicing knife with a very thin serrated blade, and a small paring knife. Buy knives in a specialty store where the selection is generally better. To select a knife, try holding a few different ones to find one that has a comfortable handle and weight. Carbon blades tend to discolor, but sharpen easily and hold a good edge.

Pots and pans: A cast-iron skillet and a nonstick skillet along with a few lidded saucepans and a larger pot for boiling pasta can easily turn out delicious, uncomplicated dishes. Glass baking dishes, pie pans, and mixing bowls are inexpensive and versatile for oven or microwave cooking. A baking sheet or jellyroll pan works for cakes and cookies. Many of my pots and pans belonged to my grandmother and they continue to work just fine, and I do a lot of cooking. Nowadays, expect to spend about $50 to $100 on basics.

Gadgets: Some gadgets make food preparation easier. Don't overlook a can opener, grater, vegetable peeler, strainer, colander, measuring cups and spoons, and garlic press preferably made of stainless steel. Many are available at the supermarket, but again, beware: Low prices sometimes mean poor quality. A sturdy, well-made garlic press is an important timesaving gadget. A good press pushes all the garlic through small holes. Cheap ones allow some of the garlic to stay on the top or sides. The best presses come from Switzerland, Italy, or France. Expect to spend $8 to $15 for a good one. Most of these bare-bones gadgets cost between $3 and $10. Remember that this basic equipment is a one-time expense.

CHAPTER 6

ABOUT RECIPES

If you give the same recipe to three people who use the exact same ingredients, you may notice that each finished dish tastes just a little different from the others. Why? Because variations in measurements, freshness, availability, cooking utensils, oven heat calibrations, weather, geography, and even mood will affect the outcome of that recipe.

Learn to trust your taste and your other senses—smell, sight, and touch. The recipes in this book are flexible; use them as a guide to personalize your food and create your own recipes. Open your refrigerator or cupboard and experiment with what's on hand to make a dish. Exact measures

TO CHEW ON

Rough Measuring Equivalents

Handful = ½ to 1 cup
Splash = 1 tablespoon
Pinch = ⅛ to ¼ teaspoon
Generous pinch = 1 teaspoon
Soupspoon = 1 tablespoon
Coffee spoon = 1 teaspoon
Coffee cup or wineglass = ¾ to 1 cup

are not always necessary; sometimes I measure ingredients with my eye and hand or a convenient spoon or mug.

Don't be hesitant to make on-the-spot substitutions to suit your taste and what ingredients you have on hand. (See the section on basic substitutions, pages 263–264.) If recipe calls for oil, butter, or margarine, try cutting the amount in half.

Loosen up in the kitchen, share kitchen chores with family and friends, and enjoy your meals.

FAST FOOD TECHNIQUES

Much is said about how little time we have to cook. Many people have given up cooking entirely, and of those who do cook, many spend less than half an hour cooking dinner. Yet it's possible to prepare fresh, nutritious foods quickly and easily. Some fresh, fast foods that can be eaten raw or take less than fifteen minutes to cook include asparagus, apples, bananas, oranges, potatoes, couscous, eggs, chicken parts, fish fillets, and ground meat and poultry. You'll find many others in the recipes in this book.

Cooking Techniques

Cooking techniques play an important part in food preparation. To save time—don't forget to use your microwave!

TO CHEW ON

Be sure to taste your dish before you serve it.

Along with cutting cooking time, the following techniques do not require much or any fat. These techniques can help you create a meal in thirty minutes or less:

Broiling: Chicken parts cook in a preheated broiler (about 550 degrees F overhead heat) in 5 or 6 minutes on each side, or until meat is done. Fish, even thicker cuts, cooks in minutes on each side. Meats such as steaks and chops also cook quickly under the broiler. Use the overhead heat to quickly brown the top of bread for garlic bread.

Poaching: Use barely simmering liquid such as water, wine, broth, or orange juice to cook chicken or fish in minutes. Use skinned chicken parts or fish fillets. Flavor the liquid with herbs, onion, or garlic, and use enough liquid to cover the food. Bring the liquid to a boil, turn to simmer, then add the food. Cover and cook.

Stir-frying: Toss or stir small pieces of food quickly in a skillet or wok on high heat. Use with little or no oil, depending on the food (fatty or lean) and whether you have a nonstick skillet or wok.

Steaming: Cook foods with steam coming from the liquid below. Small pieces of vegetables or cut up meats cook quickly. Food does not rest in the liquid, but above it.

Boiling: Lots of boiling liquid, usually water, rapidly cooks pasta, rice, lentils, beans, and vegetables.

Grilling: Grilling cuts time if you prepare the food while the coals or gas barbecue is heating up.

TO CHEW ON

Recipes are not etched in stone.

Pan frying: Cook foods in a skillet on the stove. Great for chops, steaks, and other meats with a little fat on them. Use a nonstick skillet whenever possible.

EASY ENTERTAINING AND PRESENTATION TIPS

You don't need big bucks to have a bash, just think simple, fresh, and seasonal for your menu. Here are a few of my favorite party dishes and serving tips.

- Use condiments to jazz up simply roasted, grilled, poached, or baked fish, meat, poultry, or vegetables. Some basics are mustard, ketchup, and pickle relish while more exotic accompaniments include fresh salsas and cooked chutneys. All usually have no fat, and they balance sweet, sour, and spicy flavors. Homemade salsas and chutneys make good use of a variety of fresh fruits and vegetables such as apples, pears, peaches, melons, and tomatoes.

- Think color and crunch or texture when considering fun and different ways to present your favorite dishes.

- Wrapping foods, particularly in tortillas, makes easy on-the-run meals. Other wraps include: Crunchy lettuce leaves (green), cabbage leaves (green and purple), taco shells, and soft pita and cracker breads

- Shredded carrot or cabbage or even finely chopped lettuce makes a colorful bed for salads, meats, and other vegetables.

- Open your cupboard and use a pretty glass or mug for carrot sticks, dips can go into a hollowed-out cabbage or an unusual bowl or cup.

- Everyone loves chips, but not necessarily the fat in them. Look for baked chips, particularly corn chips, that work well with nonfat salsas and bean dips. To bake your own chips, cut corn tortillas into eighths and lay them on a cookie sheet. Bake in a preheated 325 degree F oven, turning occasionally, until crisp. Serve with salsa.

- Check what is on-hand in the refrigerator. For example, leftover ricotta cheese can be mixed with a little tomato sauce or salsa, spread on crackers or bread, and broiled until the cheese gets bubbly. Or buy cans of already cooked black beans (about $.50 to $.75 each), purée, then add chopped onion, Mexican blend or cumin, and some salsa for a yummy lowfat dip.

- For a change from canned mixed roasted nuts (high in fat and salt), try toasting raw almonds (available in the bulk section of the supermarket) on a cookie sheet for about half an hour in a 250 degree F oven. These nuts have no added oil or salt, and they're terrific with drinks.

- Finger foods are fun to eat and pretty to display on a platter or in a bowl. Splurge for fresh crab (in season) or boiled shrimp served cold (with or without the shell). Serve with lemon or a lowfat mayonnaise dip. Watch for store specials to get good buys on these high ticket foods. Other finger goods include (in season): asparagus, artichokes, cherry tomatoes, and olives. Other main-course foods include simple roasted or grilled turkey, chicken served cold with greens and a zippy vinaigrette dressing, or white bean and chicken chili.

- Chocolate-dipped dried figs make an easy, tasty, and sweet nibble. Melt a little semisweet chocolate, dip the bottom of each fig in the chocolate, and cool on waxed paper. Try them with red wine or port.

FOOD PRESENTATION FOR KIDS (AND GROWN-UPS, TOO)

Whether you are a kid or an adult, how food looks affects whether or not you want to eat it. Here are a few fun ways to serve some foods:

- Use cookie cutters (hearts, animals, and other shapes) to make sandwiches visually appealing for the lunch box.

- Vary the bread you use. Try stuffing pita (pocket bread) or wrapping tortillas around everything from tuna to peanut butter and jelly.

- Rice cakes are a crunchy alternative to bread when used as a base for open-face sandwiches. They also make a good snack food instead of salty crackers.

- Jazz up the presentation of carrots, celery stalks, and other vegetables. Instead of serving vegetables whole, try cutting them in diagonal 1- or 2-inch pieces, ½-inch rounds, or even small, thin strips like matchsticks. A flavored yogurt makes a simple dip.

- Make your favorite turkey or meat loaf in muffin tins rather than one large loaf. Muffin-size meat loaf makes a perfect after-school snack . . . much more fun than a slab of loaf.

- Popcorn makes wonderful finger food. Use an air popper to cut the butter and oil usually associated with this yummy food. Read labels if using the microwave variety—there may be lots of added salt and oil.

TO CHEW ON

A reminder: All ingredients, stoves, ovens, and cooking utensils are not created equal.

CHAPTER 7

RECIPES FROM APPLES TO ZUCCHINI

APPLESAUCE AND LEMON CAKE

MAKES 1 CAKE; SERVES 12

Here's a delicious cake that drops the butter or oil in favor of applesauce for taste, texture, and moistness—without extra calories from fat. The elimination of fat in baking has a historical precedent—fruit purées were used by America's settlers during the fall and winter when butter was hard to come by. This recipe was inspired by one in the Cooking Secrets of the Culinary Institute of America. *This cake is dense and not too sweet. Try it in the morning with a cup of coffee or tea. Also good as a dessert with fruit purée or a compote of fresh fruit.*

Look for unsweetened applesauce in a jar, or, if you feel so inclined, make a batch of homemade applesauce by peeling, coring, chopping, and then cooking the apples with a little water or orange or lemon juice until soft and mushy.

3 cups unbleached, all-purpose flour
2 tablespoons baking powder
Dash salt
½ teaspoon ground cinnamon
¼ cup chocolate chips
4 eggs
1 teaspoon vanilla extract
¼ teaspoon lemon extract
1 cup unsweetened applesauce
1 cup sugar
Zest of 1 lemon

Preheat oven to 350 degrees F. Spray a 10-inch tube or Bundt pan with vegetable oil spray or coat it with butter and flour.

Sift flour, baking powder, salt, and cinnamon together into a large bowl. Add chocolate chips. In a medium bowl, beat eggs and add all remaining ingredients. Mix egg mixture into the flour mixture until well combined.

Pour batter into prepared Bundt pan and bake for 45 minutes or until a skewer or toothpick inserted in the center of the cake comes out clean. Place on a rack to cool completely before unmolding.

SERVES 4 TO 6 AS A SIDE DISH

If apples are not available, try this recipe with pears or peaches. Fresh serrano chiles are hot, hot, hot, so temper the chiles to your taste or try a jalapeño for a little less heat. Rice vinegar gives a gentler flavor than cider or white vinegar. The latter two work, though I'd substitute water for half of the vinegar for less intense vinegar flavor. No matter how you tweak the taste, this chutney should be spicy, slightly sweet, tart, and have a chunky texture from the fruit.

2 cups rice wine vinegar

¾ cup brown sugar

½ red *or* green bell pepper, seeded and diced

1 or 2 serrano peppers, *or* to taste, seeded and diced

2 tablespoons finely chopped green *or* yellow onion

½ cup raisins, optional

3 large green apples, peeled (if desired), cored, and diced

2 tablespoons fresh lemon juice, *or* to taste

In a large saucepan, boil vinegar and brown sugar until sugar is dissolved.

Add remaining ingredients except apples and lemon juice. On medium heat, boil about 8 minutes. Add apples and simmer until almost dry and apples are tender and retain their shape. Taste for correct seasoning.

Remove from heat, squeeze in lemon juice, taste for correct seasoning, cool, and serve.

CHUNKY APPLESAUCE

MAKES ABOUT 4 CUPS

Per capita, in a year, Americans consume about 120 apples (40 pounds) including processed apple products. Applesauce is one of those products and store-bought sauce can be expensive and overly sweet. Make your own sauce at home for just pennies when apples are in season during the fall and winter months. I learned to make this simple and easy applesauce from my grandmother. Use it as a side dish with meats and poultry or as a satisfying dessert served with Twice-Baked Chocolate Chip–Almond cookies (page 94). Low in fat, the sauce works well alone or topped with a dollop of ice cream or yogurt.

Cook this delicious sauce on the stove as described here or make it in the microwave oven according to manufacturer's instructions.

4 large apples, cored, peeled, and chopped
Juice of ½ lemon *or* orange
Pinch ground cinnamon
¼ cup water *or* juice
¼ cup raisins, optional

In a large saucepan toss apples with lemon or orange juice, cinnamon, and water.

Bring mixture to gentle simmer over medium-low heat. Cover and cook, stirring often, until apples soften and break down into a chunky sauce, about 15 to 20 minutes.

Remove from heat and stir in raisins, if using.

Serve cool or warm; unadorned; with lemon cookies; dolloped with yogurt, ice cream, or frozen yogurt; or sprinkled with finely chopped walnuts or almonds.

APPLE CRUNCH SALAD

SERVES 4

Make this in the fall and winter when apples are crisp and plentiful. Mix red and green apples for color, add pears, dates, or a few walnuts or almonds for texture and flavor. Try a flavored nonfat yogurt or lowfat sour cream and a splash of orange or raspberry liqueur for a refreshing snack or dessert.

4 apples, cored and diced
Juice and zest of 1 large
    orange
1 tablespoon brown sugar, *or*
    to taste
¼ cup raisins, chopped dates,
    or another dried fruit
1 tablespoon orange *or* raspberry liqueur, optional, but good

4 tablespoons nonfat yogurt
    or lowfat sour cream
2 tablespoons chopped almonds *or* walnuts, optional

Mix apples with orange juice, zest, sugar, raisins, and liqueur, if using.

Spoon into 4 bowls and top with a dollop of yogurt or sour cream and a sprinkle of nuts.

SERVES 4

May is prime time for artichokes. Whether they are boiled, steamed, microwaved, or sautéed, they are low in calories (25 for a 12-ounce artichoke), and high in vitamin C, magnesium, and folic acid. There is no fat in the vegetable—until you add the traditional melted butter or mayonnaise to dip the leaves— so go low- or nonfat with the dip, and you've got a delicious, wholesome appetizer, main course, or snack. Artichokes are especially good cold and are perfect for a picnic basket.

Look for artichokes with tightly packed leaves. Frosted tips (the blistered look) may not look perfect, but still are tender and flavorful. Artichokes can be kept refrigerated for up to two weeks if they are unwashed and stored in a plastic airtight bag.

It's an art to eat this thorny thistle—one of my favorite finger foods. I love the stem which should be cut off just before cooking. Peel it and toss it into the water to cook with the artichoke. For the dip, let your taste and imagination go and create a favorite. Simple is best. Start with low- or nonfat sour cream, mayonnaise, and/or yogurt. See Mayonnaise, pages 157–160.

4 artichokes, rinsed, with stem and lower outer petals removed
Water for boiling

Optional ingredients for cooking
1 large clove garlic, pressed
1 tablespoon olive oil
1 large pinch dried thyme, basil, *or* oregano

3 tablespoons chopped fresh parsley

Lay each artichoke on its side and trim the top of the leaves with a knife to cut off the sharp tips.

Put artichokes into a large pot, cover with water. If using the optional ingredients, mix them together in a small bowl. Gently open the top of the artichoke and push a little of the mixture down toward the choke. Cover and boil gently 20 to 40 minutes. The artichoke is done when a petal near the center pulls out easily. Drain and serve hot, warm, room temperature, or cold.

To eat, pull off a petal, dunk it into sauce or dip, and pull through teeth to remove the soft, pulpy portion of the petal. Discard the remaining part of the petal. Continue eating until you reach the fuzzy center. With a spoon, remove the fuzzy part and eat the artichoke heart.

SERVES 4

This delicious vegetable is a member of the lily family (along with leeks, garlic, and onions). It is high in vitamin C while very low in calories. Asparagus is finger food—yes, the spears are meant to be eaten with your hands. Whole spears dipped in pesto-infused nonfat yogurt (for a lowfat treat) or draped with melted butter or hollandaise sauce (for a high fat indulgence) make delicious and easy party food. Canned asparagus exists, but it does not come close to fresh in color, flavor, and texture, and it is expensive. The season for fresh asparagus is short, and the prices can be high so take advantage of lower asparagus prices during supermarket specials.

Fast and tasty, asparagus cooks in 1 to 3 minutes depending on the thickness of the spear. Cooking methods include boiling, steaming, microwaving, or stir-frying. Cooked asparagus should be just barely firm, but not limp.

Try to use freshly grated Parmesan for this particular dish. Adding other vegetables helps stretch the amount of asparagus in the dish, though using all asparagus is just fine. For a vegetarian meal, serve on a bed of rice or noodles with a salad, or use as a side dish with fish, meat, or poultry.

1 pound asparagus, cleaned, trimmed of fibrous bottoms, and cut in 1-inch pieces

1 small onion, thinly sliced

1 clove garlic, pressed

½ red, green, or yellow pepper, thinly sliced, optional (see note)

¼ cup water or chicken broth

Dash salt and pepper

2 tablespoons freshly grated Parmesan cheese

Put all ingredients except cheese into a large saucepan. Cover, bring to a boil (do not leave the kitchen!), cook for 1 minute, and turn off heat. Check doneness, and set aside for another minute if not cooked enough. Drain well. Serve sprinkled with Parmesan cheese.

Note: Look for frozen sliced peppers if fresh are not in season. Roughly half a cup is equal to half a pepper.

TO CHEW ON

"The character of the cook shows in the food . . . ."
—Madame Wong, *Los Angeles Times* interview, July 11, 1996

SERVES 4 (2 WRAPS EACH)

Consider asparagus a healthy, fast food vegetable because it's low in calories and takes just minutes to cook. This recipe makes a quick, tasty, lowfat lunch, dinner, or an unusual dish for a buffet.

Figure two spears of asparagus for each taco- or burrito-style wrap. Lowfat Jack cheese cuts fat calories, and a flavorful chunky salsa gives zip to the taco. Any leftover meat will work—use the microwave oven to reheat it before serving. Present the tacos already made or put the ingredients out for create-your-own-tacos or burritos.

8 (6-inch) corn tortillas *or* flour tortillas, warmed

2 cups leftover turkey, chicken, pork, lamb, *or* beef, shredded

1 pound asparagus, stemmed and steamed, approximately 16 spears

4 green onions, finely chopped

½ cup shredded lowfat Monterey Jack cheese, about 1 tablespoon per taco

Salsa, approximately ¾ cup, *or* to taste

For each wrap, fill 1 tortilla with a little meat, 2 asparagus spears, a little green onion, cheese, and salsa. Roll or fold and eat.

ASPARAGUS WITH GINGER AND SESAME SEEDS

SERVES 4

I love asparagus stalks cooked without much fuss or embellishment. Barely steam, stir-fry, or microwave asparagus until the stalk bends ever so slightly. Asparagus has a short growing season in the spring and may be pricey, so watch for it on special at the market.

This recipe uses stalks cut into 2-inch pieces, cooked quickly over high heat with a tiny bit of oil. It's important to constantly toss the vegetables in the pan so they don't burn. Serve on a bed of rice or noodles if desired.

1 teaspoon vegetable oil
1 small onion, thinly sliced
1 small piece fresh ginger, finely chopped, about 1 teaspoon
1 pound asparagus, cleaned, trimmed of fibrous bottoms, and cut into 2-inch pieces
¼ cup water *or* chicken broth, as needed
1 heaping teaspoon sesame seeds, toasted

In a large skillet or wok, heat oil, add onion, ginger, and asparagus. Stir-fry on medium-high heat until onion and asparagus begin to soften. If it seems the asparagus isn't cooking fast enough, add some water or broth and cover for 1 or 2 minutes. Remove cover and serve sprinkled with sesame seeds.

ASPARAGUS WITH CREAMY ORANGE-SESAME SAUCE

SERVES 4

Asparagus has no fat (unless you add butter, oil, or other fatty substances), and five unadorned spears have only 20 calories. This creamy sauce has no fat, and its pale orange color contrasts well with the green asparagus. Serve spears uncut on a plate with tips draped in sauce or prop them in a pretty glass (like flowers) with the sauce on the side for a dip. Proper etiquette allows asparagus to be eaten with the fingers, thus the sauce is put on the tips so the ends remain clear for the fingers. This recipe works well for a special Easter or Passover feast.

Remember a pound serves four. To stretch the amount of asparagus, cut the spears into three pieces. Save the heavy end of the stalk for soup, stir-fry, or even Asparagus Poppy-Seed Loaf (page 48). Be sure you don't overcook the spears, they should hold their shape and just barely bend.

My favorite way to cook asparagus is to steam/boil it in a shallow saucepan: Place the spears in the pan with a little water, about ½ inch. Cover and turn the heat to high, bring to a boil, let boil about 1 minute, check for doneness. If almost cooked, turn off heat, leave cover on, and let pan rest another minute or 2. Uncover, drain, and serve hot, cold, or at room temperature.

1 small clove garlic, pressed
1 tablespoon rice *or* cider vinegar
4 tablespoons nonfat sour cream
4 to 5 drops Asian sesame oil
Pinch sugar, to taste, optional
Dash salt and pepper, to taste

Juice and zest of 1 orange, about ½ cup juice, zest optional if not using fresh orange
1 pound fresh asparagus, cooked, see instructions above
1 tablespoon sesame seeds, toasted, optional garnish

Mix all ingredients, except the orange zest, asparagus, and sesame seeds, until well blended. Taste sauce for correct seasoning. Serve on the side or spoon over asparagus tips. Sprinkle zest and/or sesame seeds over asparagus and sauce for garnish. Serve asparagus warm, cold, or at room temperature.

TO CHEW ON

Better a man should wait for a dish than a dish should wait for a man.

—Chinese Proverb

ASPARAGUS POPPY-SEED LOAF

MAKES 10 TO 12 SLICES

Try this unusual and very tasty cake bread that uses the "other end" of the asparagus—the part that usually gets thrown out or made into soup. I adapted the recipe from one inspired by a California Asparagus Festival Cook-off finalist.

This is a moist cake with a subtle overtone of asparagus. It isn't too sweet and would work very well as an ending to any meal.

Topping

¼ cup sugar

¼ cup lightly packed brown sugar

1 tablespoon unbleached, all-purpose flour

2 tablespoons butter, softened

Loaf

2 cups unbleached, all-purpose flour

½ teaspoon salt

¾ teaspoon baking powder

½ teaspoon baking soda

¼ cup butter, room temperature

2 eggs, room temperature

¾ cup sugar

1 cup nonfat sour cream

1½ teaspoons vanilla extract

¼ cup nonfat milk

2 tablespoons poppy seeds

Zest of half a large lemon, optional—and tasty

2 cups raw asparagus ends, peeled and finely chopped

Preheat oven to 375 degrees F. Grease and flour a 9 × 5-inch loaf pan.

Combine topping ingredients and mix with fork or fingers until crumbly. Set aside.

Sift flour, salt, baking powder, and baking soda, and set aside.

In a large bowl beat butter, eggs, and sugar until well blended. Add sour cream, vanilla, milk, and poppy seeds, and mix to incorporate. Add sifted ingredients, zest, if using, and asparagus and gently mix to incorporate. Dough is somewhat thick. Place batter into the prepared loaf pan. Sprinkle with topping mixture.

Bake for 55 to 60 minutes or until a toothpick inserted in the center comes out clean. Cool and slice.

BAKED BANANAS

This self-contained fruit makes a fast, soothing dessert that is perfect for a winter dinner whether you're serving 1 or 100. Make one banana per person. Bake the bananas while the guests eat. Unadorned, the natural sweetness of bananas makes them simple comfort food. Without the optional butter, this is a fat-free dessert.

1 banana
1 teaspoon butter, optional, but tasty
Sprinkling of brown sugar, about a heaping teaspoon
Pinch of cinnamon *or* cloves, optional
Splash of orange juice, rum, *or* orange liqueur

Preheat oven to 350 degrees F.

Put unpeeled bananas in a baking dish. Bake for about 15 minutes or until skin turns black and glossy.

To serve: Split banana lengthwise and leave peel on. Dot with butter, and sprinkle with sugar, spice, and juice or liqueur.

BANANA COFFEE CAKE

MAKES 40 PIECES

What's the fruit that's always in vogue, high in potassium, and great finger food? Bananas, of course! Bananas are perfect to eat when the skin is completely yellow, but many times the skin ripens to an unappealing brownish black. Then it's time to make this yummy dense cake, which uses ripe bananas and buttermilk. The riper the bananas, the more flavorful the cake. Use all raisins or a mix of chocolate chips and raisins.

If you don't have buttermilk on hand, sour milk is an easy substitution. Make your own sour milk by adding 1 table-spoon white vinegar or lemon juice for every cup of milk. Let curdle for 5 or 10 minutes before using.

If you don't want to make the topping, toss a few nuts into the cake, rather than on top. This cake needs no mixer and can be made in just minutes. It is good solo, with fresh fruit, or even topped with a small scoop of ice cream or sorbet.

1½ cups lowfat buttermilk *or* sour milk, see above
2 teaspoons baking soda
¾ cup white sugar
2 eggs
3 ripe bananas, mashed
2 tablespoons butter, melted and cooled
¼ teaspoon ground cloves
¼ teaspoon nutmeg
1 teaspoon vanilla
1¾ cups unbleached, all-purpose flour
Dash salt
½ cup raisins

½ cup chocolate chips *or* raisins, optional

Optional Topping

¼ cup chopped almonds *or* walnuts
1 teaspoon cinnamon, if desired
¼ cup brown sugar, well packed

Preheat oven to 350 degrees F. Grease a 9 × 13-inch pan.

In a small bowl, mix buttermilk and baking soda. Let rest.

In a large bowl, with a fork or hand mixer, beat sugar and eggs until well blended. Add bananas, butter, cloves, nutmeg, and vanilla. Mix well.

Add flour, salt, raisins, and chips, if using. Blend. Add buttermilk mixture.

Pour into prepared pan. If using, combine the topping ingredients and sprinkle over the surface. Bake about 30 to 40 minutes or until a toothpick tests clean when inserted in the cake.

MAKES ABOUT 4 CUPS

Barley reminds me of hearty winter soups my grandmother used to make. But barley isn't a grain only for soup. When cooked as a side dish it becomes an economical and easy accompaniment to broiled, roasted, or grilled meat, fish, or poultry. Consider color and texture when you make this dish—frozen corn, peas, or a few sliced mushrooms make nice alternatives to the carrot and broccoli. This dish takes about 15 minutes to cook—the trick is to use boiling water. The cooked barley should be firm, not mushy.

1 tablespoon vegetable *or* olive oil

1 medium onion, finely diced

1 clove garlic, minced *or* pressed

1 cup raw barley

2 cups boiling water *or* chicken *or* vegetable broth

Salt and pepper, to taste

1 teaspoon dried Italian herb blend, *or* your favorite

1 stalk broccoli, including florets, cut into bite-size pieces

1 small carrot, finely chopped

1 heaping tablespoon grated Parmesan cheese, with additional to serve on the side at the table, if desired

In a large saucepan, heat oil and add onion and garlic. On medium heat, cook 1 or 2 minutes or until onion begins to soften.

Add barley and stir to coat with oil. Add boiling water or broth, salt, pepper, and herbs. Cover and cook on medium heat 10 minutes.

Add broccoli and carrot, stir, cover, and cook another 5 minutes. Check for doneness. Barley should be just firm and liquid absorbed. Add Parmesan, stir, and taste for correct seasoning. Serve with additional cheese on the side.

BLACK BEAN AND HOMINY SALAD

MAKES ABOUT 3½ CUPS

Fast, tasty, full of fiber, and low in fat, this salad is a cinch to make. Zip it up with lemon, orange, or lime zest (grated peel). For something different, serve the salad wrapped in warm corn tortillas with shredded lettuce, a bit of leftover roasted poultry or meat, and a splash of salsa. For crunch, celery works but isn't a must. This colorful blend of black beans and hominy (corn) makes a delicious addition to any meal, in any season.

To save money, buy dry beans at about 60 cents a pound and cook them yourself. If time is a consideration, canned beans are the ticket and cost about 60 cents for a 15-ounce can. I like to rinse the canned beans to remove the salty liquid. Look for canned hominy (white corn kernels) in the Mexican food section of the supermarket. If you don't like hominy, add corn kernels.

1 (15-ounce) can black beans, drained and rinsed
1 (15-ounce) can hominy, drained and rinsed
1 small rib celery, finely chopped
½ teaspoon ground allspice *or* cloves, *or* to taste
3 medium green onions, *or* ¼ small onion, finely chopped
Zest and juice of 1 medium lemon, orange, *or* lime

1 clove garlic, pressed
1½ tablespoons cider vinegar, *or* to taste
1 teaspoon fruity olive oil, *or* to taste
Pinch red pepper flakes, *or* to taste

Toss all ingredients in a bowl. Mix, taste for correct seasoning, and serve chilled or at room temperature.

MAKES ABOUT 2 CUPS

Great for fast, last-minute dishes, beans—white, black, kidney, pinto, garbanzo—make easy salads, sides, and dips. They have almost no fat and are high in fiber. A well-stocked cupboard always has a few kinds of canned beans on the shelf. This dish is perfect for unexpected guests. Try other varieties of beans with different combinations of herbs and spices: Black, kidney, and pinto beans love cumin, garlic, and a pinch of oregano.

1 (15-ounce) can white beans, emptied into a strainer, drained, and rinsed
1 medium clove garlic, pressed
2 tablespoons minced fresh parsley, basil, thyme, *or* oregano *or* a mix, *or* about 1 teaspoon dried
Zest or grated peel of 1 small lemon
Salt and pepper, to taste

1 tablespoon fruity olive oil, optional

Mix all ingredients and gently mash the beans for a chunky texture. For a smooth dip, purée in a food processor, adding a little water if oil isn't used. Adjust seasoning to taste, and serve with crackers or small rounds of toasted bread.

MAKES 1½ CUPS

1 (15 ounce) can black *or* pinto beans, rinsed
1 clove garlic, pressed
½ teaspoon ground cumin
2 to 3 tablespoons salsa
Dash cayenne *or* a few drops Tabasco sauce to taste

Place all the ingredients in blender or food processor. Cover and chill to meld flavors. Serve with chips (for homemade chips, see pages 33–34).

MAKES 1½ CUPS

Garbanzo beans (also called chickpeas) make delicious (and quick) dips that are great to munch with chips or fresh vegetables.

This dip works well with artichokes or other finger-food vegetables. Serve it as a lower fat alternative to the usual high-in-saturated-fat mayonnaise or melted butter–based dips. With no mayonnaise in it to spoil, the bean dip travels well for an easy do-ahead summer picnic food.

Save time and buy canned garbanzo beans or save a few pennies, and cook dry beans according to the instructions on the package. Canned or dry, these beans cost under a dollar.

1 (15½-ounce) can reduced sodium garbanzo beans, drained, reserving about ⅓ cup liquid, and rinsed

Juice of ½ lemon, about 2 or 3 tablespoons

1 small clove garlic, pressed

3 sprigs fresh parsley, finely chopped, about 2 tablespoons

1 medium green onion, finely chopped

Pinch dried oregano, *or* to taste

Salt and pepper, to taste

In a blender or food processor, add beans, reserved liquid, lemon juice, and garlic. Process until smooth. Add remaining ingredients and process just to blend.

Taste for correct seasoning. Serve separately for dipping artichoke leaves, pita bread, vegetable sticks, or crackers.

SERVES 6

Rice and beans are a staple in the South. Black-eyed peas and rice are known as hopping John in the Carolinas; black beans and rice are Moors and Christians in Florida; and red beans and rice are favored in Louisiana. Tradition says that any one of these combinations brings good luck for the New Year.

Beans belong to the legume family and are a good source of plant protein and fiber. When eaten with rice or other grains, low-cost beans become a complete protein. The best thing about most legumes is that they have no fat (unless it's added during cooking).

Canned beans may cost more but are definitely time-savers and can be substituted for the dried variety. Most recipes call for cooking the black-eyed peas with a ham hock or bacon, which adds smoke, salt, and some fat to the dish. To create an addictive dish with a smoky flavor and less salt and fat, try turkey bacon or smoked sausage instead. Make the beans and rice ahead of time, then combine when ready to serve. This is a terrific party dish.

1 cup dried black-eyed peas, rinsed and sorted (3 cups cooked)

3 cups water

1 dried hot pepper, optional

1 medium onion, chopped

⅛ pound turkey bacon *or* regular bacon, finely chopped, *or* 1 small ham hock, *or* 1 small smoked sausage, finely chopped

3 cups cooked white rice, warmed

In a large saucepan, put peas, water, pepper (if using), onion, and bacon. Bring to a boil, cover, and simmer about 1 hour or until beans are soft. Add water if necessary during cooking.

When ready to serve, add rice and mix to heat through. Serve with collard greens, steamed spinach, chard, or a large green salad.

GROUND BEEF AND LETTUCE ROLL-UPS

MAKES 4 SERVINGS

Lettuce leaves, particularly green leaf, Boston, and iceberg, make unusual and crunchy wrappers for these roll-ups. Any ground meat will work for the filling. Let your imagination guide you with your favorite stuffing and seasoning. This dish has an Asian twist in flavor and makes an easy, light summer meal.

¾ cup ground beef, pork, chicken, *or* turkey *or* substitute vegetables of choice

3 stalks celery, thinly sliced

½ green *or* red bell pepper, thinly sliced, optional

4 green onions, finely chopped

2 to 3 cloves garlic, finely chopped

½-inch piece fresh ginger, finely chopped

2 teaspoons Asian sesame oil, *or* to taste

1 tablespoon hoisin sauce, *or* to taste (available in Asian section of supermarket)

1 teaspoon soy sauce, *or* to taste

Pinch sugar

1 handful bean sprouts, coarsely chopped

3 tablespoons fresh cilantro, chopped

8 lettuce leaves, separated, washed, dried, and left whole

In a large nonstick skillet or wok, stir-fry meat with onion on high heat. For poultry with less fat, use a teaspoon or so of vegetable oil to cook. Remove meat to a strainer to drain fat. Put meat in a bowl.

Use the same skillet to stir-fry celery, bell pepper (if using), green onions, garlic, and ginger on high for 1 or 2 minutes until vegetables just begin to soften.

Put sesame oil, hoisin sauce, soy, and sugar in a small bowl and mix.

Add meat, bean sprouts, cilantro, and sesame oil mixture to vegetables. Stir-fry on medium-high heat for about

30 seconds, to mix all the ingredients. Bean sprouts should be crunchy. Taste for correct seasoning.

To serve, put filling in a bowl surrounded by lettuce leaves. Guests put a few spoonfuls of filling on a leaf, roll, and eat.

BEER AND HERB BREAD

MAKES 1 LOAF, APPROXIMATELY 12 SLICES

Serve this easy beer and herb bread as an accompaniment to meats, vegetables, or cheese. The dough is mixed with only a fork and the beer gives a slightly yeasty flavor without the hassle of proofing dried yeast. The basic recipe can be made for much less than a dollar.

Experiment by adding herbs such as oregano, basil, or dill, or toss in half a cup of corn, olives, cheese, or onion. The amount of salt called for here allows for a slightly undersalted loaf. You can relax if fat is a concern: this recipe has little of it— just watch the butter you slather on the warm bread!

1 large egg

1 (12-ounce) bottle light-color beer

3½ cups unbleached, all-purpose flour

½ teaspoon baking soda

1 teaspoon baking powder

½ teaspoon salt

1½ teaspoons ground cumin, oregano, *or* other dried herb

2 medium green onions, finely chopped

1 fresh jalapeño, finely chopped, *or* ½ teaspoon red pepper flakes

Preheat oven to 350 degrees F. Thoroughly grease a 9 × 5 × 3-inch loaf pan.

In a small bowl, beat egg with a fork and add beer. Set aside.

In another bowl, blend remaining ingredients and add beer mixture. Mix enough to incorporate, do not overblend. Dough will be thick.

Put dough in loaf pan. Bake for 40 to 50 minutes or until a knife comes out clean.

SERVES 4

If you want something swell to make with day-old bread, try French toast. Depending on the spices and herbs used, the dish can be sweet or savory. For breakfast or dessert, use eggs and milk or orange or apple juice with a pinch of cinnamon and serve with fresh fruit. For a different twist, use savory herbs such as rosemary or cumin and a pinch of garlic to make a light lunch or dinner dish. This is a great recipe for kids to make on Mother's Day.

Much depends on the type of bread you use. I like a substantial loaf, like sourdough. Raisin bread is good as is whole wheat. Try not to use a thin, light bread as it soaks up too much liquid and can tear. You don't want to have the bread soggy, dip it just enough to wet each side. Use a nonstick skillet with no or little butter, and cook on a medium-low heat so the bread won't burn. Use nonfat or lowfat milk, or if calories and fat aren't a problem for you, use half-and-half for a richer dish. The recipe below is for a breakfast or dessert toast.

3 large eggs

1¼ cups orange juice, nonfat milk, *or* apple juice

1 or 2 tablespoons sugar, *or* to taste, optional

½ teaspoon vanilla extract, optional

¼ teaspoon cinnamon, *or* to taste

Shake or two of salt

Butter, as desired, for cooking

8 slices bread

In a bowl large enough for the bread, mix with a fork the eggs, juice or milk, sugar (if using), vanilla (if using), cinnamon, and salt.

Heat a large nonstick skillet with butter (if using). Dip each slice of bread, one at a time, into the egg mixture. Let excess drain off before placing bread in the skillet.

On medium heat, cook as many slices as the skillet will hold. Turn slices as they brown. Serve with fruit, jam, honey, or syrup.

BREAD AND VEGETABLE SALAD

SERVES 4 TO 5

This satisfying, fresh-tasting, and pretty salad brightens up any summer meal. Here summer squash and tomatoes are center stage along with fresh herbs and yesterday's dry bread. Try this almost-fat-free dish with grilled fish, meat, or poultry or alone as a light summer lunch.

Quantities and kinds of vegetables and herbs may be varied according to seasonal availability and your taste. Use zucchini or some of the other small yellow and green varieties of summer squash. Steam or for added flavor, grill the squash. Cucumbers, celery, and bell peppers also make good additions. Use a good-quality country-style bread to soak up the juices. If day-old bread isn't available, cube fresh bread and lightly toast it on a baking sheet in the oven.

2 to 3 cups cooked, cooled, and drained summer squash, about ¾ pound, cut into small chunks

2 medium-large ripe, juicy tomatoes, peeled, if necessary, and cut into small chunks, juice saved

4 thick slices day-old *or* toasted country Italian bread, cubed

1 small red onion, thinly sliced

1 clove garlic, pressed

1 or 2 tablespoons fruity olive oil, *or* to taste

1 or 2 tablespoons red wine vinegar, *or* to taste

Salt and pepper, to taste

3 sprigs fresh basil, *or* to taste, leaves torn into small pieces

2 sprigs fresh parsley, thyme, *or* oregano, finely chopped, optional

1 tablespoon capers, *or* to taste, optional

In a large bowl, toss squash, tomatoes and juice, bread, and onion.

In a separate bowl, mix remaining ingredients, then toss over vegetables. Mix, taste for correct seasoning, cover, and let rest at room temperature

62 *Bread*

or refrigerate for at least 1 hour. There shouldn't be much liquid, as the bread soaks up most of it. Adjust the dressing if you want a wetter salad.

TO CHEW ON

Need a last-minute recipe or cooking instructions? Check the manufacturer's recipes on the backs of cans and packages.

BREAD SOUP WITH VEGETABLES

SERVES 6 TO 8

The Italians have a way with leftovers, particularly bread. This recipe makes use of day-old bread in a soup called ribollita *that literally means "reboiled." This is a terrific dish to make ahead and reheat. The bread is added to a hearty minestrone and then reheated to a thick mush. Perfect for a cold night's dinner or hearty lunch, it's a meal in itself that won't break a food budget. Serve with a salad and light dessert.*

It's almost impossible to miss with this soup, especially because you can't overcook it and the exact amount of each ingredient is subject to your taste. Note there are no added herbs or meat for flavor, just the aromatic vegetable mixture called odori *(finely chopped together carrot, red onion, celery, parsley, and garlic). The soup typically contains cabbage and spinach, chard, or kale along with other seasonal vegetables. Look for Progresso cannellini (large, white kidney) beans in the supermarket, otherwise use Great White Northerns.*

1 or 2 teaspoons olive oil, *or* to taste
1 large red onion, finely chopped
1 rib celery, finely chopped
1 medium carrot, finely chopped
3 medium cloves garlic, finely chopped
6 sprigs fresh parsley, finely chopped
1 (15-ounce) can tomatoes
1 can cannellini beans, drained
1 medium potato, peeled and chunked
½ head red *or* green cabbage, coarsely chopped
1 bunch spinach, chard, *or* kale, *or* a combination, rinsed, stemmed, and chopped
Salt and pepper, to taste
10 to 12 thick pieces day-old Italian bread, chunked
2 green onions, finely chopped, optional as garnish
Parmesan cheese, as garnish

In a large pot, heat olive oil. Add onion, celery, carrot, garlic, and parsley. Sauté until vegetables soften. Add tomatoes with juice, beans, potato, cabbage, and spinach or greens. Add water to cover the vegetables. Cover and cook on medium-low heat until vegetables are very soft. Taste and season with salt and pepper.

Remove from heat, add bread and cool preferably overnight.

To serve, reheat on medium-low for at least 30 minutes.

This is a thick soup. Serve sprinkled with green onions (if using) and grated Parmesan cheese on the side. A small spoonful of pesto also makes a delicious addition.

GINGERED BROCCOLI WITH SESAME

SERVES 6

If you love ginger, you'll love this dish. Though former President Bush wouldn't touch this cruciferous vegetable, broccoli is one of the healthiest foods around. It has special enzymes, good amounts of beta-carotene, vitamin C, and plenty of vitamins and minerals. This dish adds pizzazz to a simple meal of rice or noodles and poached, grilled, or roasted fish, poultry, or meat.

Be sure to use fresh ginger, which is available in the produce section of the supermarket. Ginger keeps well either frozen or refrigerated in a covered glass jar filled with white wine.

1 large bunch broccoli, about 1½ pounds
1 tablespoon vegetable oil
1 to 2 tablespoons fresh grated gingerroot, to taste
Pinch sugar, *or* to taste
¼ teaspoon sesame oil
1 tablespoon light soy sauce
¼ cup water
2 teaspoons cornstarch *or* 1 tablespoon arrowroot, dissolved in a little water
1 tablespoon toasted sesame seeds for garnish

Cut broccoli into bite-size pieces. The stalk can be included if it isn't too thick and tough. Peel a layer off, then slice it thinly.

Steam broccoli for 3 to 5 minutes or until just tender, not soft. Or cook in microwave oven according to manufacturer's instructions.

Heat vegetable oil in wok or skillet, and sauté ginger for 1 minute. Add broccoli and toss for another minute to coat the broccoli with ginger.

In a small bowl, mix sugar, sesame oil, soy sauce, and water. Pour over broccoli, stir, and continue to cook over medium-high heat for a few minutes. Stir in cornstarch or arrowroot mixture and cook, stirring, until the sauce thickens and broccoli is glazed, about 1 or 2 minutes. Garnish with toasted sesame seeds and serve immediately.

SERVES 4

Brussels sprouts take on a new look and taste twist in this flavorful side dish. Rather than appear whole, overcooked, and soggy, the brussels sprouts are shredded or thinly sliced and quickly cooked to create a delicious and easy-to-prepare dish. This dish is great with mashed potatoes and turkey.

1 cup water
1 pound brussels sprouts, ends trimmed, halved and finely sliced *or* shredded
2 large cloves garlic, finely minced, about 1 tablespoon
1½ teaspoons cumin seeds, sesame seeds (lightly toasted in a dry skillet), *or* caraway
Salt and pepper, to taste

In a large sauté pan, bring water to boil, then turn to simmer. Add brussels sprouts, and garlic. Cook uncovered over high heat, stirring often, until sprouts are crisp but soft, about 5 minutes. Add more liquid as needed. Stir in seed of choice and season with salt and pepper.

This dish could be cooked, covered, in the microwave oven according to the manufacturer's instructions. Use less water—about ½ cup.

TABBOULEH

SERVES 4 TO 6 AS A MAIN COURSE

Tabbouleh is cracked bulgur wheat salad. Bulgur is to Armenian cuisine as couscous is to Moroccan. Both grains are low cost, need only boiling water to plump up, and make delicious last-minute salads. Look for them in the bulk foods or rice section of the supermarket. Though recipes for tabbouleh salad are endless, this addictive one was inspired by my friend Nancy Mehagian. The flavors are simple and clean on the palate.

This is a fast salad to make. While the bulgur is resting, chop the veggies. Serve the salad on a platter or in a bowl ringed with lettuce or cabbage leaves. It's a perfect picnic salad that can be made a day ahead. Round out the salad with pita bread and dessert.

2 cups fine bulgur, #1 size
2 cups boiling water
1 bunch green onions, finely sliced
1 medium onion, finely chopped
1 medium bunch parsley, finely chopped
½ bunch fresh mint leaves, finely chopped
1 large cucumber, peeled, seeded, and finely chopped
2 large tomatoes, chopped
⅓ cup extra-virgin olive oil
¼ cup red or white wine vinegar
Juice of 2 medium lemons

1 tablespoon low sodium soy sauce, optional
Dash cayenne, optional
Salt and black pepper, to taste

Pour boiling water over bulgur. Let rest 5 to 10 minutes, then fluff. Add onions, parsley, mint, cucumber, and tomato. Gently toss. Add remaining dressing ingredients, toss, taste for correct seasoning, and refrigerate.

Toss and taste to correct seasoning before serving. Salad will keep refrigerated 3 to 4 days.

RED CABBAGE WITH APPLE

SERVES 4

The simplicity of this dish makes it perfect paired with roast pork or chicken. Look for cabbage at bargain prices year-round. It's a healthy food that's as good cooked for hearty winter meals as it is raw for light summer dishes.

For a richer dish, add a few teaspoons of butter when cooking. Add a discrete pinch of caraway seed if desired. This dish is meant to be uncomplicated and simple.

1 small head red cabbage, shredded
1 medium onion, finely sliced
1 apple, peeled and shredded
3 tablespoons apple cider vinegar
¼ cup apple juice
¼ cup water
2 teaspoons sugar, *or* to taste
Salt and pepper, to taste

1 tablespoon chopped fresh parsley, optional for garnish

Put all ingredients, except parsley, in a large pan. Cover and cook on medium-low heat for about 30 minutes, stirring occasionally. Cook until cabbage is soft. Serve with parsley sprinkled on top.

CABBAGE AND CORNED BEEF STIR-FRY

SERVES 5 TO 6

Rather than death by boiling, the renowned (and many times overcooked) Irish corned beef and cabbage takes a lesson from the Far East and is quickly stir-fried. The dish is lighter, faster, cheaper, and healthier than its traditional counterpart. It's a variation of the cabbage recipe on page 72. Save money and time: Buy only a few ounces of already cooked meat to flavor the dish. Less meat also means less salt and fat. With potatoes and cabbage available year-round, this is an economical (and delicious) way to feed a crowd. Use the microwave oven to cook the potatoes and this meal is on the table in less than 30 minutes.

Lettuce leaves make a fun and unusual presentation. Spread a leaf with horseradish sauce and/or mustard, add the cabbage mixture, wrap, and eat with your hands.

1 to 3 teaspoons vegetable oil
½ teaspoon caraway, seeds *or* ground *or* to taste
1 medium onion, thinly sliced
1 large clove garlic, pressed
½ green bell pepper, diced, optional
4 ounces cooked corned beef, cut in matchstick pieces
¾ head medium cabbage, shredded
1 carrot, shredded
4 to 6 medium potatoes, baked *or* boiled, cut in small chunks
Salt and pepper, to taste

1 head green leaf lettuce, washed and dried, leaves left whole

In a wok or large skillet, heat oil and caraway for 30 seconds. Add onion, garlic, and green bell pepper, and stir-fry about a minute on high heat or until onion begins to soften.

Add the remaining ingredients, except lettuce, and stir-fry about 2 minutes on high heat or until the cabbage just wilts and mixture is hot.

Serve in a bowl with lettuce leaves on a separate platter.

Variation: To serve alone, don't add the potatoes to the stir-fry. Instead, serve them boiled or mashed as a side dish, or spread potatoes on a platter and top with the vegetable mixture.

TORTILLA-WRAPPED CABBAGE AND CORNED BEEF

SERVES 5 TO 6

This dish gives an international spin to a traditional favorite. Take a hint from Asian cuisine and stir-fry the vegetables. The results are tasty and this fast cooking technique uses oil sparingly. Another Asian tip: Use meat as a condiment. Forget the idea of cooking a huge piece of corned beef for hours: have the deli of your supermarket slice a few ounces to add to the mixture. To serve, add a south-of-the-border twist and use tortillas to wrap the mixture like burritos.

I use 6½-inch tortillas and make small bundles. The quantities in this recipe are general and can be varied according to your taste and preferences. This is an easy vegetarian dish— just skip the corned beef.

1 teaspoon vegetable oil
½ teaspoon pickling spice, crushed and chopped *or* ground
1 medium onion, thinly sliced
2 cloves garlic, pressed
½ large head cabbage, shredded
1 rib celery, finely chopped, optional
1 medium carrot, shredded
3 ounces deli corned beef, thinly sliced and cut in matchstick pieces
5 medium potatoes, boiled *or* baked, cut in small pieces
6 sprigs parsley, finely chopped
1 package no-fat flour tortillas, warmed

Put oil in a large skillet, add spice, onion, and garlic. Cook on medium-high heat for a minute and then add cabbage. Stir-fry a few minutes, add remaining ingredients, except tortillas, and continue cooking until cabbage begins to wilt and mixture is hot.

To serve, spread tortilla with your favorite horseradish or mustard, then top with a few tablespoons of vegetable mixture. Wrap like an envelope and eat with your hands, or if using larger tortillas, add more vegetables, wrap like a burrito, and eat with a fork.

CANTALOUPE SALSA

SERVES 6 TO 8

Summer means salsa—fruit salsa, that is. Salsa adds few calories and lots of flavor, color, and texture to grilled meats, fish, and poultry.

Other fruits and vegetables such as mangoes, pineapple, tomatoes, corn, and black beans make easy salsas. Summer is especially good for salsas because of the abundance of fresh produce and the ease of cooking meat or fish outside on a grill.

Another plus: salsas aren't cooked, won't spoil in the heat, and contain little or no fat. To serve this salsa with meats or poultry, add a little chopped jalapeño or serrano pepper. Be sure to sample the salsa and adjust the flavors to your taste.

1 cantaloupe, peeled and diced
Juice of 2 limes
Juice of ½ lemon
Small handful fresh cilantro, finely chopped
¼ small red onion, diced
¼ red bell pepper, finely diced

Pinch salt and pepper, to taste
Dash of rice vinegar, optional, but good with fish

Mix all ingredients in a bowl. Cover and chill for 15 to 30 minutes. Taste for correct seasoning.

SERVES 4

Cinnamon gives carrots a boost in this quick-cooking dish. Carrots carry me through the winter months with a boost of vitamin A and beta-carotene. They are always a good buy.

A little butter or olive oil gives this dish a rich flavor and texture while the vinegar or lemon juice balances the brown sugar. These carrots partner well with fish, meat, or poultry, or try them as part of a vegetarian meal. To complement other dishes in the meal, add the spice or herb of your choice—kids may be partial to cinnamon.

2 teaspoons olive oil, butter, or a mix
1 small onion, thinly sliced
1 clove garlic, pressed
1 pound carrots (about 4 to 6 medium size), thinly sliced into rounds
2 tablespoons brown sugar
1 teaspoon cider vinegar *or* lemon juice
2 tablespoons water, if necessary to keep carrots from sticking
Salt and pepper
Pinch ground cinnamon, *or* to taste

1 tablespoon fresh chopped parsley

In a saucepan, heat oil and add onion and garlic. Cook on medium-high heat for a few minutes until the onion begins to soften. Add carrots, sugar, vinegar, water, salt, pepper, and cinnamon. Cover and continue cooking for about 2 or 3 minutes. Stir frequently.

Carrots should be soft, not limp. Taste for correct seasoning, and serve with parsley sprinkled on top.

CAULIFLOWER WITH ALMONDS AND RAISINS

SERVES 4 TO 6

Tired of the usual cheese sauce on cauliflower? Raisins, almonds, garlic, and a hint of cinnamon dress the cauliflower to create a veil of subtle Moroccan flavors that will garner raves—and respect—at any meal. This dish works with a side of rice or pasta and most any meat, fish, or poultry dish.

Cauliflower is a cruciferous vegetable and a relative to broccoli; both are associated with reducing the risk of cancer. When buying fresh cauliflower, look for a firm white head (known as the "curd"). There should be no brown spots, and the green leaves under the curd should not be wilted. While most cauliflower is white, there is a green hybrid called cauliflower-broccoli. Treat it the same as the white, though it does cook a little quicker. Prices fluctuate depending on the season and weather conditions.

1 medium-large cauliflower
1 tablespoon olive oil
1 large clove garlic, finely chopped
2 tablespoons raisins, soaked in water, about 10 minutes
2 tablespoons almonds, slivered *or* chopped
Salt and pepper, to taste
⅛ teaspoon ground cinnamon
1 tablespoon chopped fresh parsley, optional for garnish

Trim the stalk from the cauliflower and cut away the green leaves. Steam or blanch whole or cut into florets, on the stovetop or in the microwave oven. Don't over-cook as the cauliflower cooks again. Florets need not take more than 3 to 5 minutes to cook. If cooked whole, break into florets. Blanching in boiling water will take about 1 minute for florets and 3 to 5 minutes whole.

Heat oil in a large skillet that can be covered. With heat on medium, add the garlic and

(Continued)

cook until it turns golden, a few minutes.

Add cauliflower and remaining ingredients, except parsley. Stir, cover, and turn heat to low. Stir occasionally and cook about 5 minutes or until cauliflower is done to taste. It should not be crunchy. Serve warm with parsley sprinkled on top.

CELERY SALAD

SERVES 4

Crunchy celery makes a perfect last-minute salad. This salad can be high or low in fat calories depending on the dressing ingredients you choose. Figure one large stalk of celery per person.

Dress this dish up by sprinkling about a tablespoon sesame seeds or chopped peanuts or almonds on top before serving.

4 large stalks celery, split lengthwise and thinly sliced

2 green onions, thinly sliced, or ½ small red onion, thinly sliced

2 tablespoons finely chopped parsley, optional

3 to 4 tablespoons any combination of light sour cream, mayonnaise, or nonfat plain yogurt

1 to 2 tablespoons cider or wine vinegar, or to taste

Salt and pepper, to taste

Pinch sugar, or to taste

Dash Tabasco sauce

1 small carrot, finely shredded for color and garnish

1 tablespoon finely chopped almonds, peanuts, or sesame seeds, optional for garnish

Put celery, onions, and parsley (if using) in a bowl. In a small bowl, mix remaining ingredients, except for carrot and nuts. Add to celery and taste for correct seasoning. Serve sprinkled with carrot and nuts, if using.

SERVES 4

Fresh red or green leaf chard makes a very satisfying and quick-cooking vegetable dish. Serve it with broiled, grilled, or roasted foods or with heartier dishes. A splash of vinegar may be added just before serving, or serve vinegar in a small bowl at the table for guests to add if desired.

1 large bunch chard, red *or* green, *or* spinach, stems removed, rinsed with water still clinging to leaves, and coarsely chopped

1 large clove garlic, pressed *or* minced

Drizzle of olive oil, less than 1 tablespoon

¼ cup water

Salt and pepper, to taste

Put all ingredients in a large skillet. Cover and cook on high heat 2 or 3 minutes or until chard begins to wilt. Stir and turn heat to medium. Continue cooking a few more minutes or until chard is soft.

Serve warm or at room temperature either alone or on top of rice, beans, couscous, or bulgur.

MARCIE'S BLUE CHEESE DRESSING

MAKES ABOUT 2 CUPS

Blue cheese makes a great addition to sauces, salads, meats, poultry, and even pastas. Use it solo crumbled as a topping or mixed with mayonnaise and other ingredients for a versatile dressing. This lowfat dressing is a hit on green salads, jazzes up roasted chicken wings, works as a vegetable dip, and tastes great with pasta. If you want to serve the dressing warm as a pasta sauce, use lowfat ricotta cheese in place of the mayonnaise.

My always-try-to-have-on-hand staples include low- or nonfat mayonnaise, yogurt, ricotta cheese, and sour cream. I regularly use these lowfat foods rather than the traditional high-fat versions. While blue cheese may be on the pricey side (and it's high in fat), a little goes a long way.

¾ cup low- *or* nonfat mayonnaise

¾ cup low- *or* nonfat sour cream *or* plain yogurt *or* a mixture

1 small clove garlic, pressed

1 medium green onion, finely chopped, about 2 tablespoons *or* use white *or* yellow onion

4 sprigs fresh parsley, finely chopped, about 4 tablespoons

2 to 3 tablespoons crumbled blue cheese, *or* to taste

1 tablespoon white vinegar

1 tablespoon lemon juice

Black pepper, to taste

Dash cayenne, to taste

In a bowl, mix all ingredients. Taste and adjust seasonings. Chill and serve as a dip, dressing, or sauce.

CRISPY CHEESE COINS

MAKES ABOUT 40

Serve these crispy, cheesy nibbles with drinks. Perfect for holiday parties, make the dough ahead, refrigerate, then cut and bake when you need them.

Almost any cheese will work; about 4 ounces does the trick. My favorites are blue, Cheddar, and Parmesan. I use herb blends to flavor the mixture, though a solo herb such as rosemary, basil, oregano, or cumin is equally tasty—it all depends on your taste. Curry powder gives a zippy flavor boost and colors the dough with a hint of yellow. Add cayenne or a dash of dried red pepper flakes for a burst of heat in each bite. I use nonfat milk, though a fatter milk makes a slightly richer dough.

1 cup (about 4 ounces) grated cheese such as Cheddar, Parmesan, *or* blue
¾ cup unbleached, all-purpose flour
2 tablespoons butter, room temperature
2 tablespoons finely chopped green onions, optional
1 teaspoon Italian herb blend
Dash salt
Dash cayenne, optional
4 to 6 tablespoons milk

Preheat oven to 350 degrees F. Grease a baking sheet.

In a bowl, mix cheese, flour, butter, green onions (if using), herbs, salt, and cayenne (if using) with a fork until crumbly. Add 4 tablespoons milk and mix until ingredients begin to hold together. Add additional milk by tablespoonful if necessary to bind ingredients. In the bowl, knead the dough by hand for a minute or so. Dough should be slightly sticky.

Roll into an 8-inch log, wrap in plastic wrap, and refrigerate at least 1 hour. Dough can be frozen then slightly thawed for slicing.

Slice the dough into ¼-inch rounds. Place rounds almost touching on baking sheet.

Bake for 8 to 10 minutes or until golden. Remove from baking sheet and cool on wire rack. Store in airtight container. Serve room temperature.

TO CHEW ON

Looks can be deceiving—it's eating that's believing.

—James Thurber

CHEESY BEER BISCUITS

MAKES 20 TO 24 DROP BISCUITS

I used to think of biscuits as difficult to make. Flour flew all over my kitchen as I struggled to roll the dough. Once rolled, it stuck perfectly to the rolling pin and the floured board, and the misshapen mess never felt the heat of an oven. Then I discovered the joy (and ease) of drop biscuits. This recipe is versatile and foolproof, and these zippy little gems can be made and baked in 15 minutes with ingredients already on hand.

If using self-rising flour, omit baking powder and salt. If you don't have beer, use milk, buttermilk, or even orange juice. The darker the beer, the more intense the beer flavor in the biscuits. For more variations, add ½ to ¾ teaspoon dried herbs. For zip, add red pepper flakes, and for a richer dough, add 2 more tablespoons butter. Your biscuits will be light and tender if you work the dough quickly and gently. Serve the biscuits with any meal.

2 cups unbleached, all-purpose flour

1 tablespoon baking powder

¼ teaspoon salt

2 tablespoons butter, slightly softened

⅓ cup grated Cheddar cheese, packed

½ teaspoon dried red pepper flakes, *or* your favorite herb blend, optional

1 cup beer, milk, buttermilk, *or* orange juice

Preheat oven to 500 degrees F. Grease a baking sheet.

Place flour, baking powder, and salt in a bowl and mix with a fork to incorporate the butter until mixture has the consistency of coarse crumbs.

Add remaining ingredients and quickly mix with a fork until well blended.

Drop dough by the tablespoonful fairly close together onto prepared baking sheet, and bake for 8 to 10 minutes or until golden. Serve immediately.

CHICKEN SIMMERED IN ORANGE JUICE AND ROSEMARY

SERVES 5 TO 6

This simmered (or poached) chicken makes a refreshing and light dish. Serve it hot with rice or pasta, or lay cooled pieces on greens for a hearty salad.

If desired, this dish can be cooked in a microwave oven, just follow your manufacturer's instructions.

Salt and pepper
1 frying chicken, skinned, cut into 8 pieces, and excess fat removed
1 heaping teaspoon dried rosemary, crumbled, *or* 1 small sprig fresh leaves
1 clove garlic, pressed
1 cup orange juice
2 navel oranges, sliced
1 tablespoon chopped fresh parsley for garnish

Salt and pepper the chicken. Place pieces in a large skillet. Add rosemary, garlic, and orange juice. Bring to a boil, immediately turn heat down to simmer, cover, and cook about 15 minutes or until pieces are done.

Garnish chicken with orange slices and sprinkle with parsley. Serve with a green salad or vegetable and crusty bread.

CHICKEN SALAD BLT

6 SERVINGS

Here's a clever summer meal that combines the flavors of a bacon, lettuce, and tomato sandwich with chicken in a salad inspired by one from Carole Lalli.

Cut fat and save flavor: Trim the fat from the bacon before cooking and use lowfat mayonnaise. This is a good way to use leftover roasted or grilled chicken, but any chicken meat will do; one breast is about a pound. To save money, look for chicken breasts on special—otherwise they can be costly. Or buy a whole chicken, cook it, then use the meat for two meals. Stretch the salad by increasing the amount of lettuce.

Dressing

½ cup mayonnaise
1 tablespoon Dijon mustard
Few dashes Tabasco or similar hot pepper sauce
Salt and pepper, to taste

Salad

¼ pound bacon, diced, cooked, and drained
½ head iceberg lettuce, cut into 1-inch pieces
2 whole poached or broiled chicken breasts, cut into 1-inch cubes
2 medium tomatoes, diced, or 2 cups cherry tomatoes, cut in half

6 slices good quality bread, toasted or grilled

Combine dressing ingredients in a bowl.

In a bowl, mix bacon, lettuce, chicken, and tomatoes. Add dressing, and toss to combine. Taste for correct seasoning.

To serve: Place slices of bread on individual plates and heap salad on top to serve as open-face sandwiches. Alternatively, serve family style in a big bowl, with toasted bread on the side.

SERVES 4

Put herbs and spices under the chicken's skin before cooking so the flavors permeate the meat rather than the skin (ever vigilant of extra fat grams, most of us remember to remove the skin—crispy as it is—before eating the meat).

Create your own favorite flavors for Under-the-Skin Chicken (or turkey). This is one of mine, and it's very easy.

1 orange *or* lemon, thinly sliced

1 or 2 large cloves garlic, pressed

2 or 3 teaspoons olive oil, optional

½ teaspoon dried herbs such as Italian blend *or* single herbs such as rosemary, thyme, tarragon, *or* cumin, *or* 1 tablespoon fresh herbs such as basil *or* parsley, finely chopped

1 whole fryer, *or* 3 to 4 pounds of parts

Preheat oven to 400 degrees F.

Mix fruit, garlic, olive oil, and herbs together in a small bowl.

The trick with the chicken is to make a pocket under the skin next to the flesh.

Gently run your hand under chicken skin to loosen it from the meat. If it is a whole chicken, begin at the top of the breast and work down to the legs and thighs. Do not remove skin.

Take orange or lemon slices and gently shove them under the skin, down as far as leg and thigh. Use all slices. Any extras can go into the cavity.

For a whole chicken, roast for about 1 hour or until done. For parts, grill, broil, or bake for 10 to 15 minutes or until done.

CHICKEN SALAD WITH PINEAPPLE SWEET-AND-SOUR DRESSING

SERVES 4

For an intriguing change from the usual mayonnaise-dressed chicken salad, give this zippy sweet-and-sour dressing a try. The dressing also works nicely with leftover pork or plain boiled shrimp. Serve the salad on a bed of shredded or torn lettuce mixed with a little green or red onion or shredded daikon, carrot, or red cabbage, or even chilled cooked rice.

3 cups poached *or* plain roasted chicken picked from the bones, shredded, *or* use pork, (see note below)

1 (6-ounce) can pineapple juice

1 clove garlic, pressed

1 small piece ginger, finely chopped

½ teaspoon Asian sesame oil, *or* to taste

4 tablespoons cider *or* white vinegar, *or* mix them

3 to 4 tablespoons brown *or* white sugar

Dash dried red pepper flakes, to taste, optional

1 teaspoon soy sauce, *or* to taste

1 to 2 tablespoons chopped fresh cilantro

Put chicken in a bowl. Mix remaining ingredients sepa-rately and let stand, if time allows, to meld flavors. Pour over chicken and mix. Cover and chill. Serve on a bed of lettuce, or toss into cooked pasta or rice for a salad.

Note: To poach chicken or parts, put chicken in a large pot and cover with water. Bring to a boil, immediately turn to simmer. Skim the brown protein particles that come to the surface. Cover and simmer for 20 minutes. Remove from heat and let chicken rest in liquid, about 45 minutes. Remove from liquid, skin, and cool so meat can be pulled from bones. Use meat for salads, sandwiches, or stir-fried dishes.

HIGH-HEAT CRISPY CHICKEN WITH SPICY SAUCE

SERVES 4 TO 6

Buffalo chicken wings are a popular treat, but often very greasy. In my version, the chicken is baked at high heat, rather than deep-fried. This produces crisp chicken without the additional oil.

3 to 4 pounds chicken parts, wings, legs, *or* thighs

Salt and pepper, to taste

4 to 5 tablespoons butter *or* olive *or* vegetable oil, *or* a mix

1 tablespoon white vinegar

1 to 5 tablespoons Tabasco *or* Louisiana hot sauce, *or* to taste

Preheat oven to 450 degrees F.

Salt and pepper chicken. Bake for 20 to 25 minutes until skin is crisp and meat is tender.

In a saucepan, heat remaining ingredients.

To serve, lay chicken on a platter and pour sauce over it, or serve sauce on the side.

Celery sticks to dip in blue cheese salad dressing make a tasty accompaniment to the chicken.

CHICKEN WITH GARLIC AND VINEGAR

SERVES 4 TO 6

Jazz up a simple sauté of chicken with a splash of wine vinegar. Though it seems an unusual ingredient, the vinegar melds well with the chicken, garlic, and parsley. This quick and delicious main course goes well with rice, pasta, or bread and a big green salad.

I prefer to skin the chicken to reduce the fat and allow the flavors to permeate directly into the meat. A nonstick skillet will work with a bit of fruity olive oil to flavor the sauce. The flour on the chicken helps thicken the sauce. Wine vinegar gives a richer flavor than cider or rice vinegar, though all are tasty.

3 teaspoons olive oil

1 fryer chicken, skinned and cut up into 8 pieces *or* 3 pounds fryer parts, dredged lightly in unbleached, all-purpose flour

2 to 3 cloves garlic, finely chopped

4 sprigs fresh parsley, finely chopped, about 2 tablespoons

½ teaspoon dried tarragon, rosemary, *or* your favorite herb

Salt and pepper, to taste

⅓ cup wine *or* cider vinegar

¼ cup water

Heat a teaspoon of oil in a large skillet. Add chicken and cook on medium heat until lightly browned, about 5 minutes on each side. If necessary, cook chicken in two batches. Remove chicken to a plate. If there are lots of burned bits and pieces in the skillet, rinse it with hot water and return it to stove.

Heat skillet with another teaspoon or two of oil. Add garlic and 1 tablespoon parsley. Cook on medium heat stirring for a minute or until the garlic turns golden, not burned. Add chicken, tarragon, salt, pepper, vinegar, and water. Turn chicken to coat in the mixture. Cover, turn heat to medium low, and cook about 20 minutes or until chicken is no longer pink. Turn chicken at least once while it cooks. Add more water if necessary. Serve with remaining parsley sprinkled on top.

**MAKES ABOUT 24 MEDIUM *OR* 12 LARGE DUMPLINGS,
DISH SERVES 6 TO 8**

*Comfort food and a great cool-weather dinner, chicken and
dumplings is a mainstay one-pot dish from the American
South.*

*This technique for poached chicken is adapted from the Chinese method of cooking. Skinning the chicken before cooking
reduces the fat in the broth if you don't have time to cool the
liquid to remove the fat.*

*If you don't cook these dumplings with the poached chicken
recipe, add them to a hearty vegetable soup. They're easy to
make and use on-hand ingredients for a homey, satisfying, delicious, and budget-conscious meal. The dumpling recipe is
adapted from Bill Neal's* Southern Cooking.

*There is no added fat in these dumplings. I made them with
nonfat milk and found them tough, so for best results use
lowfat or regular milk or even buttermilk. To keep dumplings
from toughening, simmer rather than boil them.*

Dumplings

1½ cups unbleached, all-purpose flour
2 teaspoons baking powder
1 teaspoon salt
Pinch black pepper
1 tablespoon dried basil
2 tablespoons fresh, chopped parsley
2 to 3 medium green onions, finely chopped (about ¼ cup)
1 egg, well beaten

Milk, added to egg to make ⅞ cup
Poached Chicken

Sift flour, baking powder, salt, and pepper together into a bowl. Mix in herbs and onions. Make a well in the center of the dry ingredients and quickly stir in all the liquid. Do not overmix.

Drop by teaspoonfuls into simmering broth. It's okay to drop dumplings close together. Cover tightly immediately and reduce heat to low-simmer. Cook 5 to 6 minutes with Poached Chicken or until tender.

Poached Chicken

1 (4-pound) chicken, skinned if desired
1 medium-large onion, quartered
2 stalks celery, chopped
2 carrots, chopped
1 teaspoon dried thyme
1 large bay leaf
10 whole peppercorns
1 teaspoon salt
Pinch red pepper flakes
1 small onion, thinly sliced
2 carrots, thinly sliced
Salt and pepper, to taste
Dash Tabasco, *or* to taste

Put all ingredients up to and including red pepper flakes in a large pot and cover with water. Bring to a boil, immediately turn to simmer. Skim if necessary. Cover and simmer for 20 minutes. Remove from heat and let chicken rest in liquid, about 40 minutes.

Remove chicken from broth, skin if necessary, and remove meat from bones. Coarsely chop meat. Strain and reduce liquid by half.

Add remaining onion and carrot to strained broth and cook until just tender, about 5 minutes. Add chicken, salt, pepper, and Tabasco. Then bring to boil, add dumplings, simmer, and cover to cook until dumplings are tender, about 5 minutes for small ones.

ONION-SMOTHERED CHICKEN

SERVES 4

Hints of cinnamon and cumin give this dish a seductive and exotic taste usually found in Indian or Moroccan food. Shop smart and buy a whole chicken or favorite parts at under a dollar a pound. These can be cut up and skinned at home. If breast meat is your thing, take note that the price runs pretty high, though in-store specials can bring the price down. This dish is terrific served over rice or with potatoes and a simple steamed vegetable or salad.

Turkey substitutes easily in this recipe. Take advantage of the yogurt's tenderizing effect and let the meat marinate overnight. For a cooking variation, marinate the meat, then grill it. If desired, the oil, onions, bay leaf, tomatoes, and sugar can be cooked separately as a sauce. The flavors meld well when the dish is made ahead and reheated.

1 fryer, cut in 8 pieces, *or* about 3 pounds bone-in parts, skinned

8 ounces nonfat plain yogurt

½ teaspoon ground cinnamon, *or* to taste

½ teaspoon ground cumin, *or* to taste

2 cloves garlic, pressed

¼ teaspoon dried red pepper flakes, *or* to taste

1 to 2 tablespoons vegetable *or* olive oil, optional if using a nonstick skillet

3 medium onions, thinly sliced

1 small bay leaf

1 (15-ounce) can chopped tomatoes, optional if grilling chicken

Pinch sugar, if using tomatoes

Salt and pepper, to taste

2 tablespoons finely chopped fresh parsley *or* fresh cilantro, for garnish

Put chicken in a large bowl. Mix well with yogurt, cinnamon, cumin, garlic, and red pepper flakes. Marinate at least 2 hours or overnight in the refrigerator.

Heat oil in large skillet (or use nonstick pan), add onions, sauté until golden. Add chicken and cook about 2 minutes on each side to just brown the meat.

Add any remaining marinade, bay leaf, tomatoes with juice, sugar, salt, and pepper. Mix, then cover and simmer for about 20 minutes or until chicken is done. Mix in 1 tablespoon parsley or cilantro. Taste for correct seasoning and serve garnished with remaining parsley or cilantro.

TWICE-BAKED CHOCOLATE CHIP–ALMOND COOKIES

MAKES ABOUT 3½ DOZEN

Easy for the kids to make, these cookies need no mixer. The cookies are twice baked to draw off the moisture and make them hard, perfect for dunking in espresso or sweet red wine. These cookies are known in Italy as biscotti which means twice-baked.

The dough may be sticky, so flour your hands before you shape the log for the first baking. These cook slowly, though to cut time, I turn the heat to 350 degrees F, cook for about 25 minutes, cool for 5 minutes, slice, and rebake at 300 degrees F for another 20 minutes or until hard. The cookies also store well in an airtight container.

¾ cup whole raw almonds
2 cups unbleached, all-purpose flour
⅞ cup sugar
1 teaspoon baking soda
Dash of salt
½ cup chocolate chips
3 eggs
1 teaspoon vanilla
¼ teaspoon almond extract
Zest of 1 small orange, optional

Preheat oven to 350 degrees F.

Put almonds in a shallow pan and toast in oven for about 10 minutes. Cool and coarsely chop.

Reduce oven temperature to 300 degrees F.

Mix flour, sugar, baking soda, salt, nuts, and chocolate chips in a large mixing bowl.

In a separate bowl, beat eggs, vanilla, almond extract, and zest (if using). Add mixture to flour, mixing to blend, about 1 minute.

Divide the dough in half and pat each half into a log about 1 inch thick, 1½ inches wide, and 12 inches long. Place the logs at least 2 inches apart on a greased and floured baking sheet.

Bake for 50 minutes or until golden. Remove from oven.

Reduce oven temperature to 275 degrees F.

Cool loaves on wire rack for 5 minutes. Put loaves on a cutting board and with a serrated knife, cut at a 45-degree angle to make approximately 16 to 20 ½-inch-thick slices. Lay slices flat on baking sheet, and bake at 275 degrees F for 20 to 25 minutes, turning them once.

Store in airtight container.

BUNNI'S BROWNIES

Made with butter, these brownies are rich, chewy, and delicious. Make them ahead of time and freeze. As Bunni says, "They are great straight from the freezer."

1 cup butter
8 ounces unsweetened chocolate
2¼ cups sugar
5 eggs
1½ tablespoons vanilla
1½ cups unbleached, all-purpose flour
1½ cups chopped pecans *or* walnuts, optional

Preheat oven to 375 degrees F.

Melt butter and chocolate together in a double boiler. Cool.

In a large mixing bowl, beat sugar, eggs, and vanilla until cream colored and sugar is not grainy to the touch, at least 10 minutes on high. Add chocolate mixture on low. Gently fold or beat in on low speed flour and nuts (if using) until just blended. Do not overbeat.

Pour batter into a greased and floured 10 × 15-inch jelly-roll pan at least 1 inch deep. Bake for 25 to 30 minutes, or until a toothpick comes out almost clean when inserted.

Cool in pan on a rack at least 1½ to 2 hours. Cut in squares.

MAKES 20 TO 25 SMALL SQUARES

If Bunni's Brownies (page 96) are too sinful, try these soft and fudgy brownies. They are rich (but not sinful) because they contain egg whites (no yolks), cocoa (lowest in fat of all chocolate), and nonfat sour cream (rather than butter). Add a few chopped nuts on top or in the batter for crunch and flavor, if desired.

Double the recipe and bake in a greased jelly-roll pan to make at least 48 small squares.

1 cup nonfat sour cream
Scant 1 cup sugar
1¼ teaspoons vanilla
Dash salt
9 tablespoons unsweetened cocoa powder
⅔ cup unbleached, all-purpose flour
½ teaspoon baking soda
3 egg whites, beaten to soft fluffy peaks

Preheat oven to 350 degrees F.

In a bowl, beat sour cream, sugar, vanilla, and salt.

Sift cocoa, flour, and baking soda into sour cream mixture. Beat on low speed to incorporate flour. Don't overbeat and dough will be thick.

Immediately fold in egg whites and gently blend.

Pour into greased 8 × 8-inch square pan. Bake 25 to 30 minutes, or until a knife comes out clean when inserted in the middle of the pan.

Cool slightly and cut into squares.

ALMOST GUILTLESS OATMEAL–CHOCOLATE CHIP COOKIES

MAKES ABOUT 60 COOKIES

Is it possible to cut two sticks of butter in oatmeal–chocolate chip cookies to just four tablespoons and not miss the fat? I did, and my tasters loved them. I'd heard a lot about substituting applesauce for fat in baking and decided it was time to give it a try. Remember the idea is to make a tasty cookie with less fat—don't expect it to taste exactly like the cookie made with all butter. After all, butter does taste good, but for the fat conscious, these cookies are delicious.

Raisins and chocolate chips make this cookie dense and sweet. To really cut the fat, drop the chocolate chips and use all raisins. If you're feeling creative, add a little orange or lemon zest or a pinch of ground cloves.

4 tablespoons butter, softened
¾ cup well packed brown sugar
2 eggs
2 teaspoons vanilla
¾ cup unsweetened applesauce
1½ cups unbleached, all-purpose flour
1¼ teaspoons cinnamon
1 teaspoon baking soda
Dash salt
1 cup chocolate chips
1 cup raisins
2½ cups uncooked oats, quick-cooking *or* old-fashioned

Preheat oven to 375 degrees F.

Beat butter with sugar until smooth and creamy. Add eggs and vanilla, and beat well. Add applesauce and beat until creamy.

With a fork, blend flour, cinnamon, soda, and salt in another bowl. Add to butter mixture along with chips, raisins, and oats. Mix well to incorporate.

Drop by teaspoonfuls onto lightly greased baking sheet. Cookies will not spread while cooking, so if you prefer a slightly flatter cookie, gently press dough with back of spoon.

Bake for 10 to 15 minutes, or until just browned on top.

Remove from oven and let cookies cool a minute or so on the baking sheet. Then remove to a wire rack to completely cool. As they cool, they get crisper. Store in an airtight container.

CHOCOLATE FUDGE PUDDING

SERVES 9 TO 12 WHEN BAKED IN 8-INCH SQUARE PAN

Adapted from a recipe in an old James Beard cookbook, this pudding uses no eggs and little fat—the cake cooks on top and leaves a layer of fudge on the bottom. What you don't eat the first day, you can reheat a day or two later, covered, in a low oven. This is a low-cost dessert, considering most of the ingredients are on hand.

Beard's original recipe calls for the semisweet chocolate. To drop some of the fat and make a slightly less sweet cake, I substitute 3 tablespoons (1 ounce) unsweetened cocoa (1.5 grams of fat per ounce) for the ounce of semisweet chocolate (8 grams of fat per ounce). If you wish, add the nuts to the flour mixture just before beating to be baked in the pudding. Or use the nuts sprinkled on top of each serving. Serve solo or with a dollop of ice cream.

1¼ cups unbleached, all-purpose flour

¾ cup granulated sugar

2 teaspoons baking powder

¼ teaspoon salt

3 tablespoons unsweetened cocoa *or* 2 full tablespoons chocolate chips *or* 1 ounce semisweet chocolate

2 tablespoons butter, melted

¾ cup nonfat milk

1 teaspoon vanilla

½ cup brown sugar

¼ cup granulated sugar

2 tablespoons unsweetened cocoa

1 cup boiling water

¼ cup toasted almonds *or* walnuts, finely chopped, optional for garnish

Preheat oven to 350 degrees F.

Sift flour, ¾ cup sugar, baking powder, and salt together three times. If using cocoa, sift the 3 tablespoons with the flour mixture.

If using semisweet chocolate, melt with the butter in microwave oven or in a double boiler. Cool slightly then mix with milk and vanilla.

Add to flour mixture and beat well. Dough will be thick. Pour into a greased 8-cup baking dish, an 8 × 8-inch square baking pan works well.

Mix the brown sugar, remaining ¼ cup granulated sugar, and cocoa, and sprinkle over top of pudding. Then pour the boiling water over the pudding.

Bake for 35 to 40 minutes or until there is a nice crust on the top. Serve warm.

CHOCOLATE CHIP CAKE

MAKES 20 PIECES, ABOUT 2 × 1¾ INCHES

This easy-to-make lowered fat chocolate chip cake uses mostly on-hand ingredients. It freezes well for up to three months, defrosts at room temperature, and mails well for gift giving. My recipe is inspired by one from Elinor Klivans.

The cake can be made easily without an electric mixer—I used a fork and spoon.

2 cups unbleached, all-purpose flour

2 cups brown sugar, white sugar, *or* a mix

½ teaspoon ground cinnamon

4 tablespoons butter, cut into small pieces, softened

1 large egg

1 teaspoon baking soda

1 cup low- *or* nonfat sour cream

2 tablespoons milk, optional

1½ cups (9 ounces) semi-sweet chocolate chips

½ cup chopped walnuts, optional

Preheat oven to 325 degrees F.

In a large bowl, put flour, sugar, and cinnamon, and mix with a fork. Add butter and mix until butter pieces are the size of peas, about 1 minute. There will be loose flour. Mix in egg. Mixture will still be dry.

Add baking soda to sour cream. Gently mix. If the sour cream is very thick, add the optional milk. Gently stir the sour cream into the flour mixture. Add chips and nuts, if using, and mix until batter is evenly moistened. Do not overmix. The batter will be thick.

Spread batter into buttered 11 × 7 × 1¾-inch baking pan or ovenproof baking dish. Bake for about 40 minutes. Cake is done when middle is slightly soft to the touch and the edges are firm. Cool cake thoroughly in baking pan on wire cooling rack. Cut into squares.

SERVES 6—⅓ CUP EACH

Chocolate is good anytime. This mousse uses on-hand ingredients and a blender. Perfect for the kids to make ahead, it's an elegant finale to any type of meal.

Try serving the mousse in small wineglasses or espresso cups, about ½ cup capacity. Don't fill to the top. Serve with a small piece of fruit, such as a sliced strawberry, or a dollop of ice cream.

1 egg white
1 teaspoon vanilla
2 teaspoons fruit-flavored liqueur (orange *or* raspberry), optional
1 teaspoon instant coffee, decaf works fine
1 tablespoon sugar
1 cup semisweet chocolate chips

¾ cup nonfat milk, heated but not boiling

Place all ingredients except milk in a blender. Add hot milk and blend on low for about 45 seconds, or until ingredients are smooth.

Pour into 6 small cups or glasses, cover, and refrigerate for at least 3 hours.

BRENDA'S CHOCOLATE PUDDING

PUDDING MAKES 6 SERVINGS OF ABOUT ½ CUP
GLAZE MAKES ABOUT ⅝ CUP

Warm homemade chocolate pudding makes a sumptuous and simple fall dessert. This recipe comes from a book called Gooey Desserts *by Elaine Corn.*

This is one time I'd say go for the calories and serve small portions. Named for Elaine's friend Brenda, the rich pudding is easy and quick to make. Serve cool or warm (if you can wait that long).

Pudding

3 egg yolks
1 whole egg
1 cup sugar
3 tablespoons unbleached, all-purpose flour
3 rounded tablespoons cocoa
2 cups whole milk
2 teaspoons pure vanilla extract
3 tablespoons unsalted butter

Beat yolks and whole egg and set aside near stove. Whisk sugar, flour, cocoa, and milk in a medium saucepan until free of lumps. Set over medium heat and cook mixture, stirring constantly with a wooden spatula, until just under a boil.

Remove from heat, whisk a little of the hot, thick cocoa mixture into beaten eggs, then pour egg mixture back into main chocolate mixture. Whisk really well. Continue to cook over medium heat another 30 seconds to 1 minute, stirring constantly until thick.

Remove from heat and stir in vanilla and butter. If lumps form, strain into a bowl. Divide among dessert bowls or goblets, cool and cover. Eat warm or chill a few hours. Serve each portion drizzled with chocolate glaze or store-bought chocolate syrup.

Chocolate glaze

2 ounces (2 squares) semi-sweet chocolate
2 tablespoons unsalted butter
½ teaspoon pure vanilla extract

Melt chocolate and butter over low heat, stirring until smooth and completely melted. Remove from heat and stir in vanilla. Use immediately.

CHOCOLATE CUPCAKES

MAKES ABOUT 48 MINI OR 18 REGULAR SIZE

The batter for these cakes is mixed with a fork so even the kids can make them in just a few minutes. Make a batch to freeze and then they'll always be on hand for a quick snack or as an accompaniment to a dessert of fruit, sherbet, or ice cream.

Unsweetened cocoa keeps the fat calories down in this recipe. I prefer the mini-size cupcakes since one or two satisfy that chocolate urge. If you don't have buttermilk on hand, sour your own milk by adding 1 tablespoon vinegar or lemon juice to a cup of milk and letting it rest for 5 minutes, then use in recipe.

To freeze: After the cupcakes are completely cool, lay them in a single layer on a baking sheet, cover, and freeze about 1 hour. Then transfer to an airtight storage container to continue freezing. Before serving, defrost on a plate at room temperature, then dust with powdered sugar or a dollop of your favorite frosting.

1 cup sugar

2 tablespoons melted butter

3 tablespoons lowfat buttermilk

Zest of 1 orange, optional, but very tasty

1¼ cups unbleached, all-purpose flour

⅓ cup Hershey's unsweetened cocoa

1 teaspoon baking soda

Dash salt

1 cup lowfat buttermilk

½ teaspoon vanilla extract

Preheat oven to 350 degrees F.

In a large bowl put sugar, melted butter, and 3 tablespoons buttermilk. Mix well with a whisk or fork. If using zest, add it and mix.

In a small bowl, with a fork, mix flour, cocoa, baking soda, and salt.

Put ⅓ flour mixture in sugar mixture, mix slightly, and add ⅓ of remaining cup of buttermilk. Mix. Continue adding flour and buttermilk, mixing well after each addition. Add vanilla and blend.

Fill well-greased muffin tins ⅔ full. For large cupcakes, bake about 15 to 20 minutes. For mini cupcakes, bake about 8 minutes. Cupcakes are done when a toothpick comes out clean when inserted in the middle of the cupcake or the top of the cupcake springs back to the touch of your finger.

RED, WHITE, AND GREEN SALAD

*Cinco de Mayo is traditionally celebrated with foods represent-
ing the colors of the Mexican flag—red, white, and green. To go
along with the usual guacamole and other party dishes, try this
light white corn or hominy salad. It's a quick and tasty side
dish for grilled meats, poultry, or seafood. It travels well for
picnics because it won't get soggy or go bad in the heat.*

*Look for canned hominy in the Mexican or rice section of the
supermarket. Available in white or golden, hominy's a bargain at about 79 cents for a 28-ounce can. Hominy is a main
ingredient in a well-known Mexican soup called posole. Fresh
tomatillos, found in the produce section add a slightly tart
flavor to the salad. Unless an additional flavor is desired, no
oil is necessary in this very lowfat dish.*

1 (28-ounce) can white
hominy, drained and rinsed
2 small tomatillos, papery
covering removed, finely
chopped
1 large tomato, seeded and
chopped
1 handful fresh cilantro, *or* to
taste, finely chopped
½ fresh jalapeño chile, finely
chopped, (see note below)
Juice of 1 lime, *or* to taste
3 green onions, finely
chopped
Salt, to taste
2 teaspoons fruity olive oil,
optional

Toss all ingredients together,
taste for correct seasoning,
and serve.

A few tablespoons of your favorite salsa will work if
tomatoes and tomatillos are
unavailable.

Note: Remove the chile seeds
to reduce the dish's hotness.
Use gloves when handling the
chile *or* be sure to wash your
hands immediately after
working with the chile. The
oil can burn the eyes if
touched with your fingers.

CORN AND SWEET POTATO SALAD

MAKES ABOUT 4 CUPS, TO SERVE 6 TO 8

Corn and sweet potatoes partner well in this colorful, fresh-tasting summer salad. Easy to make and flexible for ingredient substitutions and personal taste, this salad can be made in just minutes. The orange-lime dressing, with no oil, makes the salad tasty, yet low in fat. It's a simple and delicious side dish for summer barbecues.

The salad is perfect for leftover white or yellow corn on the cob. Simply cut the kernels from the cob. Don't worry about exact amounts for the ingredients, you can use more or less corn depending on your leftovers. White potatoes also work well and can be combined with the sweet potato. If fresh oregano or basil is available, use it rather than the dried herb. Sprinkle a finely chopped mixture on top of the salad.

1 pound sweet potatoes, boiled or baked, peeled, and cut into small pieces
2 cups corn kernels, cooked
2 medium green onions, *or* ½ small red onion, finely chopped
1 teaspoon dried oregano, *or* to taste
Juice and zest of 1 orange, about 5 tablespoons

Juice of 1 lime, about 2 tablespoons
Salt and pepper, to taste
Dash red pepper flakes, optional

Mix all ingredients together. Taste for correct seasoning. Let rest for a few minutes to allow flavors to meld. Serve slightly chilled or at room temperature.

CORN AND TOMATO SALSA

MAKES ABOUT 4 CUPS

Salsas are to Central America what chutneys and sambals are to India and Southeast Asia—zippy accompaniments to such foods as meats, vegetables, rice, and eggs. This summer salsa is perfect with all grilled foods or as a nonfat topping for baked potatoes or even an unusual dressing for a huge green salad. Use leftover barbecued corn for the additional flavor. I used about ½ of a fresh jalapeño chile.

2 cups cooked corn kernels

3 medium-large ripe tomatoes, diced

1 tablespoon minced fresh red *or* green chile of your choice

¼ cup fresh cilantro *or* parsley, *or* a mix

¼ small red onion *or* 2 green onions, finely chopped

¼ cup fresh lime juice, about 2 limes

½ cup tomato juice, V-8, *or* Snappy Tom

Salt and freshly cracked black pepper, to taste

Combine all ingredients and mix well. The salsa will keep, covered and refrigerated, for 4 or 5 days.

CORNED BEEF AND CABBAGE SALAD

SERVES 4 TO 6

I love corned beef sandwiches—once a year. This dish takes the flavors of the sandwich and makes a salad with less meat, more cabbage, and a zippy horseradish dressing. Use already cooked deli corned beef to cut time.

1 medium to small head cabbage, red, green, *or* a mixture, about 1½ pounds
2 stalks celery, thinly sliced
4 green onions, finely chopped, *or* ¼ small onion, finely diced
1 to 2 cups chopped cooked corned beef, about ⅓ to ½ pound
6 tablespoons nonfat *or* light mayonnaise *or* nonfat yogurt, *or* a mix
1 heaping tablespoon ketchup
1 teaspoon mustard, if desired
2 teaspoons bottled horseradish, *or* to taste, drained
2 tablespoons finely chopped fresh parsley
Salt and pepper, to taste
4 slices rye bread, crusts removed, cubed and toasted, *or* about ½ cup boxed croutons

In a large bowl, put cabbage, celery, onion, and corned beef.

In a small bowl, mix remaining ingredients, except bread. Toss with cabbage mixture. Taste for correct seasoning. Serve topped with croutons.

EASY CORNED BEEF HASH

SERVES 4

Here's another quick recipe that uses already cooked deli corned beef rather than the huge slab of meat you cook forever at home. Corned beef hash isn't only for breakfast. Serve this hash for dinner using a bed of quickly stir-fried cabbage to give a little crunch and make a pretty presentation.

Cabbage and potatoes tend to be good buys, especially during the winter and store specials. You may pay a little more for deli corned beef, but you also won't have to use much, and there is no waste. This recipe was inspired by numerous ones by James Beard.

Hash recipes generally tend not to have exactly measured ingredients so feel free to create your own balance. I prefer more vegetables than meat. Adding a little cream or water as the hash cooks makes a wonderful crust.

For the hash
½ pound cooked corned beef, sliced and chopped, *or* bits and pieces
6 to 8 medium potatoes, peeled, boiled, and chopped
1 large onion, finely chopped
Pinch nutmeg
Freshly ground pepper and salt, to taste
2 tablespoons oil *or* butter for cooking

For the cabbage
1 small head red *or* green cabbage, finely shredded

1 small carrot, shredded
1 small onion, finely sliced
Drizzle of oil for cooking

Combine all hash ingredients except oil in a bowl. Blend well and let rest in refrigerator overnight or for a few hours.

To cook, heat a large heavy skillet, nonstick if desired, and put a drizzle of oil on the bottom. Add the hash and press down. Cook on medium heat until hash begins to crust on the bottom. With a spatula, gently lift and turn so bottom crust is brought to the top. You can add a little boiling water or cream to help the crust form more quickly. Cook and turn several times to allow the crust to form.

To make the cabbage, heat a skillet and toss all ingredients on medium-high heat until wilted but with a little crunch left, about 2 minutes.

To serve, place the cabbage on a platter and top with the hash, crust side up.

BASIC POLENTA

SERVES 4

When I think of comfort foods, my favorites include—not necessarily as a complete meal—roasted chicken, steamed artichokes, and polenta, better known as coarsely ground cornmeal. Polenta is a versatile staple in Italian cooking. It cooks in 20 minutes and can be served in a variety of ways. Serve it soft right from the pot or let it cool on a sheet or in a loaf pan, slice, then broil or fry it. Basic polenta takes well to hefty tomato, meat, or pesto sauces or simple additions of Parmesan or Gorgonzola cheese.

Use broth to make a richer dish. To avoid lumps in the cornmeal, add it very slowly to the simmering water or broth, and stir constantly. I recently served this dish with a bottled tomato sauce to which I added a few sliced and sautéed mushrooms. The meal included a salad and bread and it took less than 30 minutes to make.

Look for cornmeal in the bulk or grain section of the supermarket—it's always a bargain.

6 cups water *or* broth
2 teaspoons salt, *or* to taste
½ teaspoon dried herbs such as Italian blend, basil, *or* rosemary, optional
Scant 2 cups coarsely ground cornmeal

In a large saucepan, bring liquid, salt, and herbs to a boil. Turn heat to simmer and slowly add cornmeal. Stir constantly as you add the polenta.

Continue to stir the mixture, which will slowly thicken. The mixture is done when it begins to pull away from the sides of the pot.

Serve immediately on a platter topped with your favorite sauce, sausages, or cheese.

CORNMEAL AND BLUE CHEESE SQUARES

MAKES 20 SQUARES

Try this tasty cornmeal (polenta) appetizer for a Superbowl Sunday party. It's easy finger food that has an unusual zip from the blue cheese. Cornmeal is inexpensive and available in the grocery store, boxed or in bulk. Polenta goes well as a side dish with meats and poultry.

Chicken stock adds richness. If blue cheese isn't a favorite, use ½ cup Parmesan or other cheese. If you want to forget the cheese, add a tablespoon of dried Italian herb seasoning. Try not to add the cornmeal too quickly or it may get lumpy. Keep the heat at a simmer so the mixture doesn't spatter.

1 tablespoon olive oil
1 onion, chopped
1 clove garlic, pressed
6 cups water *or* chicken stock, *or* a mixture
3 sprigs parsley, finely chopped
½ teaspoon salt, *or* to taste
Black pepper, to taste
2 cups coarsely ground cornmeal
2 ounces blue cheese, crumbled
Dash Worcestershire sauce

Heat olive oil in a large pot. Add onion and garlic, and sauté on medium heat until onion begins to soften, about 2 minutes.

Add liquid and bring to a boil. Turn heat to simmer and add parsley, salt, and pepper. Slowly, in a thin stream, add cornmeal. Stir constantly until thick. As cornmeal begins to pull away from sides of pan, add blue cheese and Worcestershire sauce. Continue stirring to mix in the cheese. Total cooking time should be about 20 minutes.

Pour into greased 11 × 15-inch pan and spread evenly. Let rest for 15 minutes.

Cut into squares, diamonds, or cookie-cutter shapes, if desired. Serve warm. Can be made ahead and reheated quickly under the broiler.

MAKES 1 LOAF, APPROXIMATELY 10 SLICES

Corn bread is a staple on tables around the world. Whether it's served plain or flavored with jalapeño chiles, Parmesan cheese, or bacon grease, the bread is a hearty addition to a meal. Look for low-cost cornmeal in the bulk section or baking section of the supermarket. This recipe was adapted from one by Joyce Goldstein.

This easy (you don't need a mixer) recipe makes a dense loaf, with good corn flavor and a faint tartness due to the yogurt. It will store well for a few days when wrapped in aluminum foil. Serve it at room temperature or toasted.

¾ cup unbleached, all-purpose flour
2 teaspoons sugar
2 teaspoons baking powder
1½ teaspoons salt
1 cup finely ground yellow cornmeal
1 egg
1¾ cups nonfat yogurt *or* sour cream, *or* a mixture
3 tablespoons olive oil
1 teaspoon Italian herb blend, dill, *or* your favorite herbs

Preheat oven to 425 degrees F.

Butter a 5 × 9 × 3-inch loaf pan.

Sift flour, sugar, baking powder, and salt into a large bowl. Add cornmeal and mix.

In another bowl, beat egg and yogurt, and stir in olive oil and herbs. Gradually add wet ingredients to flour mixture, stirring constantly. Mix until well blended and smooth, but do not overmix.

Pour batter into prepared pan and bake for 20 to 30 minutes or until top is golden. Remove from oven and let rest in pan for 5 minutes. Turn out onto wire rack to cool completely.

ORANGE-RAISIN COUSCOUS PIE

SERVES 8

For something different, try this dessert made with couscous. The tiny semolina grain combines with hot fruit juice, orange zest, dried fruit, and spices for a light and delicious ending to any meal.

Look for couscous in the rice and grain or bulk section of the supermarket. If orange juice isn't available, try apple juice. Use a microwave oven, if desired, to boil the liquid. Vary the dried fruits to include such favorites as figs, dates, and prunes, or a mix.

For presentation, if desired, sprinkle a few tablespoons of chopped almonds, pistachios, or walnuts on top of the entire pie or serve a few whole nuts on the plate with the dessert. A dollop of flavored whipped cream or a small scoop of ice cream adds flavor . . . and calories.

2½ cups orange juice
Zest of ½ orange, finely
    chopped
½ cup raisins, *or* other dried
    fruits, as desired
¼ teaspoon ground cinna-
    mon
¼ teaspoon ground cloves
½ teaspoon vanilla extract
Dash salt
1 cup uncooked couscous
1 tablespoon orange liqueur,
    optional

In a large saucepan, boil orange juice, zest, and raisins for about 2 minutes. Turn to simmer, cover, and cook another 3 to 4 minutes.

Add cinnamon, cloves, vanilla, and salt. Simmer a minute or so and add couscous. Stir and cook about 3 minutes or until mixture begins to thicken.

Remove from heat and pour into a 9-inch pie pan that has been rinsed with water and drained but not dried. Smooth top, sprinkle with liqueur (if using) and cool. The mixture sets up rather quickly and can be refrigerated. I found it best served at room temperature.

ITALIAN COUSCOUS SALAD

MAKES ABOUT 5 CUPS

Tired of cooking during the hot summer? If so, try this yummy vegetable salad that blends two cultures: Moroccan couscous and Italian seasoning. Add a confetti of fresh raw seasonal vegetables and serve on a big bed of greens along with crusty bread and dessert for a satisfying, easy summer meal.

Couscous is a semolina grain that rehydrates with hot liquid in less than ten minutes. Look for couscous in the bulk food or grain section of the market. In bulk, it's about a dollar a pound, and a pound will make many meals. Any boiling liquid will work, including water or broth.

Because juicy, ripe tomatoes aren't always readily available in the markets, I decided to use tomato juice for the liquid. It produces a delightfully colored couscous that makes a pretty backdrop for the shredded summer veggies. If tomatoes are ripe and juicy, use a few chopped and make the couscous without the tomato juice. The touch of vinegar rounds out the flavors without the use of oil.

Note: *Follow package instructions for the amount of liquid used with the couscous. Usually, 1 part dry to 1 part liquid— though some varieties are 1 part dry to 2 parts liquid. I found that with tomato juice, it is necessary to add ¼ cup for each ½ cup liquid. Also note that tomato juice can be salty, so be sure to taste the salad before adding salt.*

1 cup dry couscous
1½ cups tomato juice
1 clove garlic, pressed
1 teaspoon Italian blend herbs
3 medium zucchini, shredded
½ medium red onion, chopped

6 sprigs parsley, finely chopped
1 small cucumber, peeled, seeded, and chopped, optional
1 medium carrot, shredded, optional

1 small green, red, or yellow bell pepper, thinly sliced, optional
Salt and pepper, to taste
2 to 3 teaspoons cider or wine vinegar, or to taste

Put couscous in a large bowl.

Put tomato juice, garlic, and Italian blend in a saucepan (or microwave oven) and bring to a boil. Immediately pour over couscous, mix, cover, and let rest for 10 minutes.

Add remaining ingredients, mix well, taste, cover, and refrigerate for at least an hour. Serve on a bed of chopped lettuce.

SERVES 6

For a fast and satisfying dish that needs no cooking, I turn to couscous, the semolina pasta that's a mainstay of Moroccan cuisine. Look for packaged couscous in the rice section of the supermarket. The couscous swells when added to hot liquid and is ready to eat in less than 10 minutes. It tastes good cold, as a salad or warm as a side dish, stuffing, or bed for grilled or boiled foods. For something different, present the salad (yellow from the curry powder) on a bed of finely chopped red cabbage or finely shredded carrot.

Couscous is versatile because it takes well to different spices and vegetables and makes a colorful addition to any meal. Vary the spices and vegetables according to seasonal availability and to complement the other dishes in the meal. This colorful recipe uses curry for seasoning, but other blends, including Italian, Mexican, or even a bit cumin and cinnamon, work well. For a heartier meal, add leftover cooked meat or poultry.

Note: *Be sure to follow the package instructions for the ratio of liquid to couscous as it varies with the manufacturer. Some instructions include use of the microwave oven.*

4 cups water, lowfat chicken broth, *or* vegetable broth

1 medium onion, finely chopped

2 teaspoons chopped fresh ginger, *or* to taste, optional

2 cloves garlic, finely chopped

2 teaspoons curry powder *or* any other herb blend, *or* to taste

Salt and pepper, to taste

2 cups dry couscous

2 cups cooked vegetables such as corn, peas, broccoli, spinach, *or* a blend

½ cup raisins, optional

3 tablespoons chopped peanuts *or* almonds

Green onion, finely chopped, optional for garnish

Few sprigs parsley *or* cilantro, finely chopped, optional for garnish

In a large pot put liquid, onion, ginger, garlic, curry powder, salt, and pepper. Bring to a boil, remove from heat, add couscous, vegetables, and raisins (if using). Mix, then cover for 5 to 10 minutes or follow package instructions. Taste for correct seasoning.

Before serving add nuts and sprinkle with chopped green onion, parsley, or cilantro. Serve hot or cold.

CRANBERRY-APPLE NO-BAKE PIE

SERVES 8

Just in time for the holidays, here is a recipe for a quick cranberry no-bake pie, which uses a graham cracker crust. Only the cranberries and apple are cooked. Make your own crust or use a premade one from the store. Pricewise, a three-pack package of graham crackers costs anywhere from $1.45 to $2.00 while the prepared crust averages about $1.35. Use fresh cranberries that are available in the winter or freeze a few packages and make the pie anytime during the year. The pie will serve eight easily.

Use regular, lowfat, or nonfat sour cream or yogurt. The choice is yours. I like to mix ½ cup nonfat yogurt with ½ cup lowfat sour cream. Sweetness is also a matter of personal taste. Here I use only a tablespoon of sugar because the apple, raisins, and juices add texture and sweetness to the tart cranberries.

This dessert is fast and easy to prepare. The fruit mixture takes only a few minutes to cook on the stovetop or in a microwave oven following the manufacturer's instructions. Make the pie the day you wish to serve it. Decorate it with fresh orange slices, if desired.

½ cup *each* nonfat yogurt and lowfat sour cream, *or* a cup of either

1 tablespoon sugar, *or* to taste

¼ teaspoon *each* vanilla and lemon extract, *or* ½ teaspoon of either

1 (8-inch) graham cracker pie crust

1 (12-ounce) package fresh cranberries

1 medium pippin apple, finely chopped

½ cup raisins

½ cup orange *or* apple juice

1 teaspoon cinnamon, *or* to taste

1 tablespoon sugar, *or* to taste

In a bowl, mix yogurt and sour cream, sugar, and extracts. Pour into prepared crust and smooth it to make a bed for the fruit. Refrigerate while fruit cooks and cools.

Place cranberries, apple, raisins, juice, and cinnamon in a saucepan. Bring to a boil and immediately turn to a simmer and cook until berries begin to pop. Taste for sweetness and add sugar to taste. Cook a few more minutes, stirring, until apples just soften. Cooking should take no more than 8 to 10 minutes. Remove from heat and cool.

When cool, pour into prepared crust and refrigerate or serve immediately.

SAVORY CRANBERRY STUFFING LOAF

SERVES 12

One of Thanksgiving's main dishes—as traditional as turkey and pumpkin pie—is stuffing. The variations on this dish are endless: The base may be bread, rice, or corn bread, and the possible additions run the gamut from fruit to nuts.

When I have the luxury of lots of time to spend cooking, I make the bread crumbs myself. Otherwise, to save time, I like to use a prepared corn-bread stuffing mix (Mrs. Cubbison's is my choice) and then add my personal touch. During the holidays, the price of a stuffing mix is generally less than that of a large loaf of bread and I can add whatever ingredients I want to make the dressing fit my meal.

Rather than stuff the turkey, I like to present the dressing as a loaf on a serving platter garnished with parsley or finely shredded red cabbage. Precut the slices for easier serving.

Other serving possibilities include packing the stuffing into muffin tins for individual servings or making it in a ring mold and serving it like the loaf. As far as additions, consider the possibilities: raisins, apples, garlic, oysters, mushrooms, parsley, orange zest, nuts, or pineapple.

This can be made ahead a day, then cooked the day of the dinner.

4 tablespoons butter, melted, or oil

1 medium onion, finely chopped

3 medium stalks celery, finely chopped

⅔ cup fresh cranberries, coarsely chopped

1¾ cups orange juice, broth, or water

1 box seasoned corn-bread stuffing

Preheat oven to 350 degrees F.

Heat butter in large skillet. Add onion and celery. Cook

on medium-high heat for a minute to soften vegetables. Add cranberries and juice. Bring to a boil, cover, and turn heat to simmer for 3 minutes. Remove from heat, add stuffing, and mix well.

Pack stuffing into well-greased loaf pan, cover, and bake for about half an hour. For crisper top, remove cover for additional 5 to 10 minutes.

CRANBERRY-APPLE UPSIDE-DOWN CAKE

MAKES 12 SMALL OR 9 LARGE SQUARES

Fresh cranberries are a delicious addition to salads, stuffings, and desserts. Buy them during the holidays when the prices are low and freeze them to use during the year. This tasty Cranberry-Apple Upside-Down Cake takes just minutes to prepare and can be made with frozen or fresh cranberries.

White sugar works, but brown sugar gives a richer flavor. Serve the cake alone, with a small scoop of ice cream, or with a dollop of whipped cream.

½ cup packed brown sugar
1 apple, cored and thinly
　　sliced
1 cup cranberries, fresh *or*
　　frozen
1½ cups unbleached, all-
　　purpose flour
½ cup granulated sugar
2 tablespoons softened butter
1½ teaspoons baking powder
Dash salt
Zest of 1 orange, optional
½ teaspoon ground cinnamon
¼ teaspoon ground nutmeg
　　or cloves
¾ cup skim *or* lowfat milk
½ teaspoon vanilla
1 egg

Preheat oven to 350 degrees F. Grease an 8 × 8-inch square baking pan.

Sprinkle ¼ cup brown sugar on bottom. Scatter the apple and cranberries over the sugar and sprinkle the remaining ¼ cup brown sugar on top.

In a bowl, mix flour, granulated sugar, and butter with fingers or a fork until crumbly. Add remaining ingredients and mix well.

Pour mixture over fruit and bake for 35 to 40 minutes or until a toothpick inserted in center comes out clean.

Run a knife around the edge of pan to loosen cake. Invert onto a serving plate. Leave pan over cake for a few minutes. Remove pan and serve warm or at room temperature.

CUCUMBER SALAD

SERVES 6

Try this easy recipe during the summer when cucumbers are plentiful and cheap. Sprinkle the cucumbers with salt to remove some of the water in them so that when they are dressed, they don't exude liquid and dilute the dressing. Do this if you wish to make the salad ahead of time to keep for a day. After the slices are rinsed, try a salad spinner to quickly dry the pieces. You can skip the salting if you dress the cucumbers just before serving. For additional crunch and color add a sprinkling of finely shredded red cabbage.

Salad

2 large cucumbers, *or* about 1½ pounds, peeled, cut lengthwise, seeded if desired, and thinly sliced *or* finely chopped

Salt

1 large carrot, shredded

1 tablespoon finely minced, fresh parsley for garnish

Dressing

2 tablespoons herb vinegar, *or* to taste (your choice)

1 tablespoon Dijon mustard

2 teaspoons sugar

4 to 5 tablespoons vegetable oil, *or* to taste

2 teaspoons dried thyme, celery seed, *or* dill

Freshly ground pepper, to taste

Put cucumbers in large bowl, sprinkle generously with salt, and let stand for 15 minutes.

Place salted cucumbers in a colander or large strainer, rinse salt off under cold water, drain, and let dry.

In a bowl, combine vinegar, mustard, sugar, 1 teaspoon oil, thyme, and pepper. Whisk ingredients and slowly add remaining 5 teaspoons oil while continuing to whisk until the mixture thickens to almost a mayonnaise consistency. Taste for correct seasoning.

Toss dressing with the well-drained cucumbers and carrot. Serve sprinkled with a bit of finely minced parsley.

(Continued)

Dressing Variation

Here is a sweet, pungent, and spicy alternative.

5 tablespoons sugar
1 cup boiling water
½ cup white vinegar
½ teaspoon salt, *or* to taste
2 fresh serrano chiles, seeded and finely chopped, or dash dried red pepper flakes, to taste
2 green onions, finely chopped

Dissolve sugar in boiling water. Add remaining ingredients and pour over cucumbers and carrots. Let cool and serve.

LEMONY LIGHT COOKIES

MAKES 30 COOKIES

This recipe uses on-hand ingredients, contains no fat, and is a cinch to make. Serve these cookies with fresh fruit or sandwiched with ice cream. These were inspired by a recipe from Maida Heatter.

2 large eggs
1 teaspoon vanilla extract
1 cup granulated sugar
Zest *or* grated peel of a lemon
  or orange, about 2 teaspoons
1½ teaspoons baking powder
1¾ cups sifted unbleached,
  all-purpose flour

Adjust rack to the middle of the oven and preheat to 375 degrees F.

In a medium bowl, beat eggs, vanilla, and sugar at high speed for a few minutes until the mixture is pale and thick enough to form a ribbon when beaters are raised. Then, on low speed, add zest, if using, baking powder, and flour, and beat only until incorporated.

Drop by rounded tablespoonfuls (or teaspoonfuls) on cookie sheets lined with baking parchment or with aluminum foil, shiny side up. Keep shapes neat and round, not ragged. Place cookies about 1½ inches apart. Shape remaining batter on parchment or foil, then slide onto a baking pan to bake.

Bake one sheet at a time for 11 minutes, turning baking sheet once to ensure even baking.

When done, the cookies will be a pale sandy color and dry and firm on top but soft as macaroons on the inside.

Let cool 1 or 2 minutes on the foil, then remove with a metal spatula to cool on racks. Store in airtight container. Served within a day or two, they retain their moist inside. For a crisper cookie, wait a few days to serve . . . if they last that long!

ANGEL FOOD CAKE

**MAKES 1 FULL-SIZE CAKE THAT SERVES 12
OR ABOUT 28 BABY ANGEL CAKES**

Angel food is my cake of choice because it is a delicious no-fat dessert. Made with the egg white rather than the fatty yolks, angel food cakes are light and take well to saucy additions of berries, peaches, or other summer fruits.

Use mini angel food cake pans, large muffin tins, or medium muffin tins (as I did to make the 28 baby angels). For something different, fold in a cup of berries or puréed fruit to the batter. Remember when separating eggs, be sure to put whites in a clean bowl, and when beating them, allow no water, fat, or other substances in the bowl or they won't whip properly. For best results, use eggs that are room temperature. If you don't want chocolate, leave the cocoa out, though the chocolate-fruit combo is quite yummy. Unbleached flour gives a slightly denser cake than does cake flour. When baking, be sure to use ungreased pans or the cake won't rise.

¾ cup sugar
¼ cup unsweetened cocoa, optional
1 cup cake flour *or* unbleached, all-purpose flour
1½ cups egg whites, about 10 large whites
1½ teaspoons cream of tartar
Dash salt
1 teaspoon vanilla extract
½ teaspoon almond, lemon, *or* vanilla extract
½ cup sugar
1 cup fresh berries *or* fresh fruit purée, optional

Preheat oven to 350 degrees F if making one large cake or 325 degrees F if making mini cakes.

Sift together 4 times the ¾ cup sugar, cocoa (if using), and flour. If you don't have a sifter, put those ingredients in a bowl and mix with a whisk or fork.

In a large mixing bowl, beat egg whites until foamy. Add cream of tartar, salt, and extracts. Beat at high speed with an electric mixer until whites are in soft peaks. Gradually add remaining ½ cup sugar, and beat until soft, floppy peaks are formed. Do not overbeat.

Sift ¼ of flour mixture over egg whites and fold into batter, about 15 strokes. To fold: use a large spoon or rubber scraper to cut down through mixture, then lift up and fold over. Do not stir or beat with mixer! Repeat with remaining flour, ⅓ at time. If adding berries or puréed fruit, gently fold them in now.

Pour batter into ungreased 10-inch tube pan or mini angel food cake pans or muffin tins. If using smaller pans, fill to almost full.

Bake about 30 minutes for large cake or about 15 to 20 minutes for smaller cakes. When done, top should be golden and spring back slightly to the touch.

Cool pan upside down for at least 1½ hours. Run a knife around the edges to loosen and remove from pan.

Serve with fruit, a drizzle of fruit purée or chocolate sauce, or alone. Store well covered.

COCONUT MACAROONS

MAKES ABOUT 40 COOKIES

You don't have to celebrate the Jewish holiday of Passover to enjoy these easy and tasty macaroons. One of my favorite cookies, they are made with no flour or leavening and are suitable to eat during the week-long holiday when leavened foods are prohibited. This recipe is adapted from one by Susan Friedland.

Unsweetened coconut may be difficult to find. If you can't, use Bakers sweetened coconut found in the supermarkets and cut sugar by half. My fondest memories of macaroons are as a soft cookie (cook at a higher heat for a shorter time), not a hard meringue (cook at lower heat for a longer time). Either way, they are delicious.

My favorite nonstick baking liner is Von Snedaker's Magic Baking Sheet available by mail at 12021 Wilshire Boulevard, Suite 231, Los Angeles, California 90025, (310) 395-6365.

3 egg whites
½ cup sugar
¼ teaspoon lemon extract
2 cups (6 ounces) finely grated unsweetened coconut

Preheat oven to 275 degrees F. Line 2 cookie sheets with baking parchment or use non-stick baking liner.

Beat egg whites until foamy. Gradually add sugar, and beat until eggs are stiff and shiny. Add lemon extract, and gently fold in coconut. Mix just to combine.

Form macaroons with 2 teaspoons or use a pastry bag and place on sheet.

Bake for 45 to 60 minutes or until macaroons are lightly colored. This makes a harder, meringue-type cookie.

I prefer a soft macaroon and bake them at 325 degrees F

for exactly 20 minutes or until tops are just golden.

Cool and remove from paper. Cool completely and store in airtight container where they will keep for several days. These cookies also may be frozen.

MAKES 30 TO 40 COOKIES

These melt-in-your-mouth ethereal mounds of beaten egg white and sugar make a delicious sweet served alone or with fruit. The same caveats for egg whites mentioned in the Angel Food Cake recipe, page 130, hold true for these cookies. Brown sugar gives a faint caramel color. Note: Without the chips or nuts, these cookies are fat free.

2 large egg whites, about ¼ cup
⅛ teaspoon cream of tartar
Dash salt
¼ teaspoon vanilla, lemon, or almond extract
½ cup white or brown sugar
¼ cup chocolate chips, optional
¼ cup chopped almonds or walnuts, optional

Preheat oven to 225 degrees F for crunchy exterior and soft interior or to 250 degrees F for chewy cookies.

Beat egg whites until foamy. Add cream of tartar, salt, and extract. Add sugar 1 tablespoon at a time and continue beating until whites form soft, billowy, almost stiff peaks. If using chips and nuts, fold them in.

Drop by tablespoonfuls on ungreased, lined baking sheet. Bake for 1 hour or until done. For chewy cookies bake for 1 hour. Cool and store in airtight container.

Note: Use parchment paper or Von Snedaker's reusable Magic Baking Sheets, 12021 Wilshire Boulevard, Suite 231, Los Angeles, CA 90025, (310) 395-6365.

PEANUT MACAROONS

If you love peanuts, you'll love these easy macaroons. Give them as holiday gifts or save them for treats at home. This recipe is adapted from a well-researched and very informative book call The Christmas Cook: Three Centuries of American Yuletide Sweets *by William Woys Weaver. These cookies were eaten in the 1850s— the original recipe is from* The Practical Cook Book *by Mrs. Bliss, printed in 1850.*

Weaver suggests using blanched (skinned), unsalted, peanuts that are vacuumed-packed in jars. A pound jar costs about $2.25 and I used the dry-roasted variety. This recipe makes a cookie that is crisp like a meringue. For a slightly softer cookie, use an additional ¼ cup peanuts and 2 more tablespoons flour.

1 pound blanched, unsalted, dry-roasted peanuts

4 tablespoons unbleached, all-purpose flour

5 egg whites, beaten to stiff peaks

2 cups sugar

Preheat oven to 250 degrees F.

In a food processor, chop peanuts to coarse meal texture, using pulses. Add flour and pulse to combine thoroughly.

Fold sugar into beaten egg whites, then add peanuts and combine.

Drop batter by heaping teaspoonfuls on baking sheets lined with ungreased baking parchment. Bake for 40 to 45 minutes or until light brown. Remove from oven and cool slightly on the paper. Then remove to cool completely on a rack.

Pack the cookies for storage in an airtight container— moisture may soften them.

BASIC CREAM-PUFF DOUGH

MAKES 2 CUPS DOUGH, ABOUT 36 TO 40 SMALL PUFFS

The French call this dough pâté à choux *(pronounced "pat a shoe") and you might think this recipe is complicated and time-consuming. Well, think again. If you want to make versatile cream-puff shells—big or small—to fill with anything from chocolate whipped cream to herbed cream cheese, try this easy recipe. All you need is butter, eggs, and flour: The dough is basically a very thick white sauce into which eggs are beaten. Make the shells small for bite-sized tidbits to serve with drinks, or larger to fill with creamed chicken or fish for a lunch, or fruit for dessert.*

For a dessert dough, use only a pinch of salt and a teaspoon of sugar. To make cheese puffs, add a cup of grated cheese to this basic dough. The more flavorful the cheese, the less you need. Herbs can be added to the dough for additional variations.

While the pastry bag makes perfectly formed puffs, I prefer to drop the dough by the teaspoon or tablespoon onto the buttered baking sheet. The trick to keep the puffs from becoming soggy is to prick the small puffs and slit the large ones immediately after they are cooked so that the steam can escape from the inside.

1 cup water
6 tablespoons butter (¾ stick)
1 teaspoon salt
1 cup sifted unbleached, all-purpose flour
4 large eggs

Preheat oven to 425 degrees F.

In a medium saucepan, bring to boil the water, butter, and salt. Boil until butter is melted.

Remove from heat and immediately add the flour. Beat well with a wooden spoon to blend thoroughly. Return to medium-high heat and continue beating until the mixture leaves the side of the pan and forms a mass. The bottom of the pan will begin to have a film on it.

Remove pan from heat and make well in the dough. Break an egg into the well and begin beating with the wooden spoon until it is absorbed into the paste. Add remaining eggs one at a time the same way. Be sure all the paste is well-blended and smooth.

Drop dough by heaping teaspoonfuls about 1½ inches apart onto buttered baking sheets. Bake for about 20 minutes or until puffs have doubled in size and are firm and crusty to the touch. Remove from oven and pierce side of each with a toothpick or sharp knife. Cool on rack.

Shells can be made ahead and frozen. To freeze: Cool completely, lay on cookie sheet in single layer, cover, freeze for 1 hour, and then transfer to plastic bags or containers. Freeze until needed. Reheat in a preheated 425 degree F oven for 3 or 4 minutes to thaw and crisp.

MAKES ABOUT 1 CUP

Though I usually count fat grams religiously, there are times that I want an elegant butter-rich lemon sauce for poached eggs, vegetables, fish, or poultry. The sauce is hollandaise, and it's a cinch to make with a blender or food processor.

This isn't everyday eating, and a little goes a long way, so consider the sauce a splurge calorically. It's perfect for a special dinner party. Try a little on the tips of asparagus, or smear a generous tablespoon on a plate and top with a piece of poached fish or poultry, or drizzle it over poached eggs Benedict.

Gear the sauce for your taste: Two yolks makes a thick, slightly yellow sauce; one whole egg and one yolk a slightly runny, light-colored sauce; and one whole egg makes a similar slightly runny, light sauce. Unsalted butter allows you to salt for taste and makes a thicker sauce. For more punch, add a dash of dried or Dijon mustard.

Be sure the butter is hot and foamy and slowly add it to the blender. If the sauce separates, add a tablespoon of boiling water and quickly reblend. The sauce can be frozen and reheated over a double boiler.

1 whole large egg
1 to 2 tablespoons lemon
    juice, *or* to taste
Dash cayenne powder *or*
    Tabasco sauce, *or* to taste
¼ teaspoon Dijon mustard,
    or to taste, optional
Salt to taste if using unsalted
    butter
1 stick butter, melted to foamy

Put everything but the butter in a blender. Blend on high for a few seconds. With the machine on, add the hot butter very slowly in a thin drizzle. As you finish adding the butter, the sauce will be done. If not totally emulsified, blend a few seconds more. Serve warm.

MAKES ABOUT 12

Crepes, those versatile thin pancakes, make perfect wrappers for fillings—from asparagus to zucchini, Roquefort to ricotta, fish to beef, and apples to strawberries.

Tricks for good crepes include allowing the batter to rest an hour after mixing and cooking in a barely greased, moderately hot pan. A thick batter yields heavier crepes, while a thin batter makes more and lighter crepes. Egg size and milk fat content may affect consistency. After batter has rested, adjust consistency by adding a tablespoon or two of milk or flour.

1 cup nonfat *or* lowfat milk
3 large eggs
1 cup unbleached, all-
    purpose flour
Dash salt
1 tablespoon sugar (if using
    crepes for dessert) *or* to
    taste, optional
1 to 2 tablespoons butter

Beat milk and eggs with a fork or wire whisk. Add flour, salt, and sugar (if using). Beat until smooth. Cover tightly and let batter rest 1 hour or overnight in refrigerator.

If batter separates, stir before cooking. Heat a 6- to 8-inch skillet (nonstick, if desired) on medium heat. With a wadded paper towel, take a small bit of butter and wipe pan to lightly coat surface. Sprinkle pan with a few drops of water; when they sizzle, the pan is hot.

Pour 2 to 3 tablespoons batter in pan and quickly swirl to evenly coat surface. If necessary, pour off excess batter. Let cook until light brown, about 30 seconds. Gently turn with a spatula, or lift a corner and flip with fingers and cook another 15 to 30 seconds.

Remove to a plate and continue cooking and stacking crepes. It may take 1 or 2 crepes to get the heat correct.

Unfilled crepes may be refrigerated for 2 or 3 days or frozen.

SERVES 6

Leftovers make great second meals. This recipe melds leftover ham (or any other meat) and asparagus (or other vegetable) with eggs for an easy frittata, also known as an open-faced omelet. The dish is inexpensive and, with a salad and bread, works for a last-minute meal, bag lunch, or light supper.

If cholesterol and fat are a problem, then use fewer egg yolks and a nonstick skillet. Use your imagination as well as your leftovers to add versatility to this dish. The quantities are loose for the meat and vegetables, though I used one large egg per serving. Make the frittata ahead of time and serve at room temperature, if desired.

1 tablespoon olive oil
1 small onion, finely chopped
6 eggs, beaten
3 tablespoons finely chopped parsley
1 cup, approximately, leftover ham *or* other meat, chopped bite size
2 cups cooked asparagus *or* other vegetable, chopped bite size
Salt and pepper, to taste
1 clove garlic, pressed
2 to 3 tablespoons Parmesan cheese, optional

In an 8-inch nonstick ovenproof skillet, heat oil and quickly sauté onion about 1 minute on medium heat, just to soften.

Blend eggs with 2 tablespoons parsley and remaining ingredients and pour into skillet. Cook slowly on medium-low heat, stirring frequently, until eggs begin to set. Cook top by placing skillet under broiler for 1 or 2 minutes to brown. If a broiler is not available, cover the skillet on the stove and cook for a few minutes so the top sets, though it won't brown.

Cut in wedges, sprinkle with remaining 1 tablespoon chopped parsley, and serve hot from the skillet or at room temperature.

SERVES 4

Eggs make a quick, comforting, and satisfying meal any time of day. This tasty, colorful dish combines crunchy vegetables with scrambled eggs. Serve with steamed rice or crusty bread, salad, and dessert to round out this low-cost repast.

Snow peas and mushrooms can be expensive. Thinly sliced, a few go a long way to add color, texture, and flavor to a dish. Use a nonstick skillet to minimize the need for oil. If desired, use three egg yolks and seven whites to cut the cholesterol.

1 tablespoon, approximate, vegetable oil

2 medium green onions, finely chopped

1 small piece fresh ginger, finely chopped

1 clove garlic, finely chopped

2 medium mushrooms, thinly sliced

6 snow peas, strung and cut lengthwise into slivers

1 cup leftover cooked chicken *or* meat, chopped, optional

1 heaping cup bean sprouts

Dash Worcestershire sauce

Dash Asian sesame oil, optional

Salt and pepper, to taste

6 eggs, beaten

Few sprigs cilantro *or* parsley, finely chopped, optional for garnish

In a large nonstick skillet, heat oil and add onions, ginger, and garlic. Stir-fry on medium-high heat about 1 minute. Add mushrooms and snow peas, and stir-fry another 30 seconds. Add meat (if using) and bean sprouts, and stir-fry another 30 seconds. Turn heat to medium low.

Mix Worcestershire sauce, sesame oil (if using), salt, and pepper with eggs, and add to vegetables. Stir to incorporate and cook slowly, stirring, until eggs are set to desired doneness. Serve sprinkled with chopped cilantro *or* parsley.

SERVES 4

For an easy meal, any time of the day, think about eggs. This dish takes scrambled eggs and embellishes them with vegetables— leftovers work well. Nickname the dish [your name] Special. Seasoning can be anything from Italian to Mexican to Indian. I use a Mexican blend here, and serve the dish with tortillas.

Vary ingredients and seasoning to your taste. To watch fat calories, use a nonstick pan, with a drizzle of oil, if desired. If vegetables aren't already cooked, cook them in their own juices rather than butter or oil. For cholesterol watchers, use more egg whites than yolks, or define the dish with more vegetables and fewer eggs. Think about color and texture also as I've done here with the addition of leftover corn from the cob.

8 eggs, well beaten

1 large clove garlic, pressed

2 teaspoons Mexican herb blend, *or* to taste

Salt and pepper, to taste

1 teaspoon olive oil

1 medium onion, finely chopped

1 medium bunch spinach, washed, stemmed, and coarsely chopped, *or* 1 package frozen, cooked according to package instructions and squeezed dry

1 cup corn, leftover corn from the cob works well, *or* use frozen kernels

3 sprigs fresh cilantro *or* parsley, finely chopped

Mix eggs, garlic, herbs, salt, and pepper in a bowl. Let rest while cooking vegetables.

In a large nonstick skillet, heat oil and add onion. Cook on medium heat a few minutes until onion begins to soften. Add spinach and toss until it begins to wilt, about 1 minute.

Add corn and egg mixture, and cook on medium-low heat stirring frequently until eggs have reached desired doneness. Serve with a sprinkle of chopped parsley or cilantro.

FAST FISH SALAD

Serve this Mediterranean-inspired, barely vinegared cold fish salad for dinner as a small first course. Present the individual portions on a lettuce leaf. Snapper or salmon (richer flavor) both work well. Cook fish in a microwave oven, poach it in water with herbs, or grill it.

2 cups cooked fish, flaked, about ¾ pound

2 small green onions, finely chopped

1 to 2 tablespoons red wine vinegar, *or* to taste

Pinch of sugar

1 teaspoon fruity olive oil, *or* to taste

Salt and pepper, to taste

¼ cup raisins

2 tablespoons raw almonds, finely chopped and toasted

With a fork, gently mix all ingredients except almonds. Taste for correct seasoning. Flavors should be gentle, not overpowering. Chill.

To serve, mound about ⅓ cup mixture on individual plates each lined with a lettuce leaf. Or, serve family style in a lettuce-lined bowl. Sprinkle almonds on top.

SERVES 6 TO 8

Perfect for kids to make, this dessert takes just minutes to prepare. Look for juicy summer fruits or low-priced peaches, nectarines, and apricots at farmers' markets or the supermarket. Serve this warm or at room temperature. Add calories with a dollop of whipped cream or a scoop of ice cream. If it's winter, use frozen berries or peaches from the supermarket.

Most any fruit will work, with the exception of pineapple and strawberries. Try to mix berries with other fruit. Look for ripe juicy fruit for more flavor. If desired, make the dessert in individual ramekins.

2 pounds fruit, such as peaches *or* nectarines, peeled, if desired, and sliced, about 2 cups

2 or 3 tablespoons sugar, *or* to taste, depending on sweetness of fruit

2 tablespoons orange juice

Zest of half an orange

2 tablespoons butter

3 tablespoons brown sugar

⅓ cup unbleached, all-purpose flour

Dash salt

½ teaspoon cinnamon

½ teaspoon dried ginger powder, optional

Preheat oven to 350 degrees F. Lightly grease a 9-inch pie pan.

Mix fruit with sugar, juice, and zest. Spread into pan.

Put remaining ingredients in a bowl. With hands, rub to crumbs. Sprinkle evenly on fruit.

Bake for 20 to 25 minutes or until bubbly and slightly browned on top.

FRUIT PUDDING

SERVES 6 TO 8

A juicy finale to any meal, this pudding works well in winter with apples or pears, or in summer with nectarines, peaches, plums, or any combination. It needs no mixer and can be done at the last minute and served warm. The crust comes up from the bottom during the cooking to make a cracked surface. If you enjoy very sweet desserts, add a little more sugar, but I rely on the fresh fruit and the orange juice for most of the sweetness.

Don't expect a typical thick pudding. The dessert is runny from the juices of the fruit. It can be a bit messy and may drip a little in the oven. Serve warm unadorned or add a dollop of ice cream or whipped cream.

1 cup unbleached, all-purpose flour
½ cup white sugar
1½ teaspoons baking powder
Dash salt
½ teaspoon cinnamon
½ teaspoon ground cloves, optional
1 teaspoon grated fresh ginger, optional
1½ cups thinly sliced fruit such as peaches, nectarines, plums, *or* apples
½ cup lowfat milk
1⅓ cups orange juice
Zest of ½ orange, optional
½ cup brown sugar
1 tablespoon butter

Preheat oven to 350 degrees F.

Grease an 8 × 8-inch pan.

Sift flour, sugar, baking powder, salt, and spices in a large bowl, or mix them all with a fork.

Add fruit and milk, mix with fork. Batter will be thick. Put into prepared pan.

Heat remaining ingredients in microwave oven or in a saucepan just to melt butter. Pour over fruit mixture. Bake for 30 to 40 minutes. Dough will rise to top of fruit. Serve warm.

MAKES ABOUT 3 DOZEN

Biscotti, the twice-baked Italian cookies you see all the time in coffeehouses, are a cinch to make. Usually the cookie includes almonds or hazelnuts and is sweet. This recipe takes the biscotti concept and creates a savory cookie to serve with drinks or snacks.

If you prefer rosemary, substitute it for the cumin seed. Parmesan may be substituted for the Cheddar cheese. If you want to cut a few minutes from the cooking time, do the first bake at 350 degrees F for about 25 minutes, then rebake at 300 degrees F for another 20 minutes. Cook less time during the second bake if you want a softer cookie.

2 cups plus 2 tablespoons unbleached, all-purpose flour
4 tablespoons sugar
¾ teaspoon baking soda
1 teaspoon whole cumin seeds
½ teaspoon dried oregano, crushed
¼ teaspoon red pepper flakes
1 clove garlic, pressed
½ cup grated sharp Cheddar cheese
2 eggs, lightly beaten

Preheat oven to 300 degrees F.

Grease and flour a baking sheet.

In a medium bowl, mix all ingredients with a fork. It will take about a minute to incorporate the dry ingredients with the egg. Dough will be stiff.

Divide the dough in half. On prepared baking sheet, form 2 logs by patting each half into a log about ½ inch thick, 1½ inches wide, and 12 inches long. Leave about 2 inches between the logs.

Bake for about 50 minutes or until just golden. Cool on wire rack for 5 minutes. Then slice each log with a serrated knife. Cut at a 45-degree angle to make ½- to ¾-inch-thick slices. You should get 16 to 20 pieces. Lay slices flat on baking sheet and recook at 275 degrees F for 20 to 25 minutes. Turn once. Cookies should just barely be hard. Cool and then store in airtight container.

TO CHEW ON

Everything you see,
I owe to spaghetti.

—Sophia Loren

FRESH BASIL PESTO

MAKES ABOUT 1½ CUPS

Pesto in its traditional form is a luscious blend of fresh basil, garlic, olive oil, and grated Parmesan and Romano cheese. The sauce livens up pastas, breads, meats, vegetables, eggs, dressings, and dips. This sauce must be made with fresh basil—dry will not work. The addition of parsley helps keep the sauce green. Many recipes call for a few tablespoons of pine nuts, walnuts, or almonds, but I prefer the sauce unadorned. For a less fat sauce, substitute chicken broth for some of the oil. Adjust the exact amounts to your taste— more cheese or less garlic, for example.

Try nontraditional pestos made with cilantro, parsley, or spinach substituted for the basil. Grow your own basil or buy it fresh during the summer months. Make a big batch (do not add cheese) and freeze pesto for use during the winter. Add cheese after defrosting.

2 cups fresh basil leaves

3 sprigs parsley, leaves only

1 tablespoon pine nuts *or* walnuts, optional, *or* to taste

2 to 3 cloves fresh garlic, peeled

6 to 8 tablespoons olive oil, *or* use part chicken stock

4 tablespoons grated Parmesan cheese

2 tablespoons grated Romano *or* Parmesan cheese

Salt and pepper, to taste

In a blender or food processor, process basil, parsley, nuts (if using), and garlic. Slowly add oil. Mix in cheeses by hand for a rough texture or incorporate them in the processor for a smoother sauce. Taste and adjust seasonings and add salt and pepper, if necessary.

SERVES 4

Jicama (the j is pronounced like the h in "hiccup") is a root vegetable that substitutes for canned water chestnuts and makes terrific salads and snacks. I love to serve it cut in sticks, either plain with a dip such as pesto-flavored yogurt or sprinkled with lime juice and a dash of chile powder. When shopping for jicama, look for firm, unblemished roots. Peel jicama, then cut or shred it.

1 small jicama, about 1 pound

1 small carrot, finely shredded

1 tablespoon salad oil, *or to taste*

2 tablespoons rice vinegar

1 teaspoon dark Asian sesame oil

Salt and freshly ground black pepper, to taste

2 teaspoons toasted sesame seeds

Peel jicama and cut into 2-inch sticks. In a bowl, mix the jicama and carrot.

In a small bowl, combine salad oil, rice vinegar, sesame oil, and salt and pepper. Taste to correct seasoning.

Pour dressing over vegetables, mix, taste again, and serve sprinkled with sesame seeds.

CURRIED CHICKEN SALAD WITH LENTILS

SERVES 4

Leftover chicken or turkey languishing in the refrigerator makes a perfect ingredient for a salad. This lowfat rendition departs from the traditional mayonnaise-based salad and uses curry powder, ginger, and garlic to jazz up the chicken. Lentils are a good source of fiber with almost no fat grams to count and run less than a dollar a pound in bulk or packaged. Green lentils cook quickly and hold their shape. Cooked red lentils tend to lose their shape; they're better for purées than salads.

Use roasted, broiled, poached, or grilled chicken or turkey. You can easily adjust the salad according to the amount of chicken you have. Use this recipe as the base for your own improvisation—add a handful of broccoli or corn for more color, texture, and fiber. Nonfat sour cream can be substituted for the yogurt, if you have it on hand, but it won't have the same tartness. You can make the parts of this salad ahead of time, mix, and refrigerate.

½ cup nonfat yogurt
1 teaspoon curry powder
1 clove garlic, pressed
1 heaping teaspoon chopped fresh ginger
Salt and pepper, to taste
½ carrot, finely chopped
2 cups cooked chicken *or* turkey, cut into bite-size pieces
1 cup dry brown *or* green lentils
1 clove garlic, pressed
Juice of 1 small lemon *or* orange (about 2 tablespoons), *or* to taste

Zest of 1 small lemon *or* orange, optional
½ small head red cabbage, finely shredded, *or* lettuce, torn into small pieces
1 tablespoon chopped fresh parsley *or* cilantro

In a medium bowl, mix yogurt, curry powder, 1 clove garlic, ginger, salt, pepper, carrot, and chicken. Cover and refrigerate.

Meanwhile, put uncooked lentils in a medium saucepan, rinse, and cover with water.

Add garlic, bring to a boil, turn heat to medium, and cover. Cook for 15 to 20 minutes or longer as necessary until lentils are soft, not mushy, and still have their shape. Drain, if necessary, and set aside.

Mix lentils with chicken mixture. Taste and add lemon or orange juice, adjust seasoning, and refrigerate to meld the flavors. Serve cold over a bed of cabbage or lettuce, topped with zest and chopped parsley or cilantro.

LENTIL PURÉE

Lentils are a versatile and inexpensive staple for Indian, Middle Eastern, African, European, and, more recently, American cuisines. They are an ancient agricultural crop frequently mentioned in the Bible. The legume is a good source of plant protein (an incomplete protein unless served with a grain or small amount of animal protein) and is low in fat.

This purée takes minutes to make. Use it warm as a side dish or serve cold as a dip with tortilla chips or pita bread. Look for red, green, or brown lentils. The red ones cook in about 10 minutes and are good for purées and soft dishes. The brown and green ones hold their shape for soups and salads but also work as a purée. They take about 20 minutes to cook. Ground spices, including curry, work with the dish and can be added to taste.

1 cup red, green, *or* brown lentils
1 medium onion, quartered
1 large carrot, thinly sliced
3 cups water
1 bay leaf
½ teaspoon mustard seeds
½ teaspoon cumin seeds
2 cloves garlic, peeled
Salt and pepper, to taste
2 teaspoons cider *or* white vinegar, *or* to taste
Dash red pepper flakes, to taste, optional
1 to 2 tablespoons finely chopped fresh parsley *or* cilantro, for garnish

In a large pot, put all ingredients except salt, pepper, vinegar, red pepper flakes, and parsley. Cover and bring to a boil. Turn to medium-low heat and cook for 10 minutes (red lentils) or 20 minutes (green or brown lentils), or until soft.

Purée in food processor. Add salt, pepper, vinegar, and red pepper. Taste for correct seasoning.

Serve hot or cold sprinkled with parsley or cilantro.

FIESTA LIMA BEAN AND CORN SALAD

MAKES 4 TO 5 CUPS

Make this refreshing and colorful dish the night before a picnic. It travels well without refrigeration because there's no egg or mayonnaise in the dressing to spoil. This salad is low in cost and fat while high in fiber and taste. The dish works well with grilled meats, poultry, and fish.

Adjust the salad ingredients to seasonal and market availability as well as to suit your taste. For added color, taste, and texture, try a little chopped green or red pepper, or a few thinly sliced red radishes. Limes give a nice fresh flavor, but orange juice can be substituted.

3 cups frozen lima beans, cooked according to package instructions

2 ears fresh corn, cooked and kernels removed, *or* use 1 cup frozen kernels

½ medium red onion, thinly sliced, *or* 2 green onions, finely chopped

¾ teaspoon Mexican herb blend, *or* to taste

Dash Tabasco sauce, to taste, optional

4 tablespoons fresh lime juice

Salt and pepper, to taste

2 teaspoons fruity olive oil

Few sprigs cilantro *or* parsley, finely chopped, about 2 tablespoons

1 clove garlic, pressed, optional

1 small carrot, shaved into ribbons with vegetable peeler, *or* shredded

Mix all ingredients in a bowl. Taste for correct seasoning. Chill and serve.

FRIED MATZO

One of the mainstay foods of the Jewish Passover holiday is matzo. It takes the place of leavened breads during the week-long Spring celebration. But you don't have to wait for Passover: Matzo is available year-round and works great for dips. It's also delicious slathered with butter and honey.

Matzo makes an easy breakfast meal when it's softened and cooked with beaten eggs. Most recipes for fried matzo call for breaking up the large squares and soaking them until mushy. This recipe is from my mother who likes her matzo whole and with texture. Whatever your preference, the orange juice and zest give it a little extra zip.

Figure one large matzo square and egg per person. If you prefer it less eggy, or are watching fat and cholesterol intake, cut the number of eggs used or use more egg whites than yolks.

½ cup nonfat milk
Juice and zest of 1 medium
    orange, *or* ½ cup orange
    juice
1 teaspoon vanilla
Dash salt
4 whole squares matzo
4 eggs, *or* 2 whole eggs and 2
    whites, beaten
1 to 4 tablespoons butter, de-
    pending on cooking
    preference

Heat milk, orange juice, zest, vanilla, and salt. Do not boil.

Lay matzos in a large baking dish. Pour milk mixture over matzo and let soak a minute. Turn matzo so liquid gets to each one. Matzo should hold its shape and not be mushy. If you'd prefer matzo in smaller pieces, break it before soaking.

Pour milk mixture into eggs. Mix.

Heat butter in large nonstick or cast-iron skillet. Add 1 matzo and pour a little egg mixture over it. Cook on medium heat long enough for eggs to just set, turn, and cook 1 minute more. If necessary, keep warm for a few minutes in a 200 degree F oven. Serve with honey or cinnamon and sugar.

MATZO SALAD

The springtime holiday of Passover commemorates the exodus of Jews from Egypt. The foods of the week-long holiday revolve around matzo, the unleavened bread eaten on the journey from Egypt because there was no time to bake leavened bread. This salad is a takeoff on the Italian bread salad, panzanella. Joan Nathan inspired this dish.

The original salad called for chicken fat. As I made the salad again and again, I found that the vinegar with just a touch of olive oil, or even no oil, was just as satisfying—with no saturated fat. The salad will be somewhat dry and that's why the vegetables are important. You don't want the matzo soggy—it should have a crunch to it when served with brisket or chicken to soak up their juices.

5 matzos

1 large green onion, or ½ medium red onion, finely chopped

2 ribs celery, finely chopped

1 teaspoon Italian herb blend

1 cucumber, peeled, seeded, and diced

2 tablespoons finely chopped parsley

6 black olives, or to taste, finely chopped, optional

2 teaspoons capers, or to taste

4 to 6 tablespoons vinegar

1 to 3 tablespoons fruity olive oil, or to taste, optional

Salt and pepper, to taste

Preheat oven to 300 degrees F.

With your hands, crush matzos into small pieces about the size of coins. Spread on a baking sheet and toast in oven for about 10 minutes, turning once in a while. Remove from oven, and put in a large bowl.

Add remaining ingredients and mix well. Taste and adjust seasoning. Salad should be crunchy, not soggy.

NONFAT THOUSAND ISLAND DRESSING

MAKES ABOUT 1½ CUPS

Homemade dressings take minutes to prepare, are less expensive than store-bought, and can be tailored to your needs and tastes.

Lettuces, tomatoes, onions, peppers, radishes, seafood, and chicken make great bowl-mates when tossed together in various combos for a hot summer mainstay—the salad. Versatile and health-friendly, salads make fast, satisfying meals. Dressings play a big part of the salad, and if you're counting calories, that's where they can quickly add up.

This mayonnaise-based Thousand Island dressing (similar to a Louis or Russian dressing) draped on a wedge of head lettuce or drizzled over seafood creates a luscious mouthful, and best of all, it's nonfat.

2 hard-boiled egg whites, finely chopped
1 cup nonfat mayonnaise
⅓ cup chili sauce
1½ tablespoons drained sweet pickle relish
1 medium green onion, minced
1 clove garlic, minced

Salt and pepper, to taste
Pinch sugar, if desired
1 to 2 tablespoons nonfat milk

Combine all ingredients except milk in a bowl. Stir in enough milk to thin to desired consistency. Taste for correct seasoning.

THOUSAND ISLAND DRESSING

MAKES ABOUT 1½ CUPS

Here is another variation for Thousand Island Dressing. This dressing is similar to Louis dressing (as in the famed crab Louis salad). Make it lowfat, if you wish, by using lowfat or nonfat mayonnaise.

1 cup mayonnaise
½ cup chili sauce
1 tablespoon finely chopped pimiento
1 tablespoon grated onion

¼ small green pepper, finely chopped
Salt and pepper, to taste

Mix all ingredients together. Taste for correct seasoning.

MAKES ABOUT 1⅓ CUPS

As a dip this sauce jazzes up cooked shrimp or chicken and can also be used as a marinade. Remoulade sauce, in a myriad of variations, has southern roots and typically is served with cooked shrimp.

Fine-tune the flavors to your taste. I used Morehouse horseradish-mustard. Tarragon vinegar works well; if you use it, leave out the dried tarragon.

2 cups lowfat mayonnaise
4 tablespoons horseradish mustard
6 tablespoons white wine vinegar
1 teaspoon dried tarragon
1 clove garlic, pressed
2 tablespoons ketchup
Pinch sugar, *or* to taste
1 tablespoon paprika
¼ teaspoon cayenne, *or* to taste
1 rib celery, finely chopped, or ½ teaspoon celery seed
1 small onion, finely chopped
1 tablespoon lemon juice, *or* to taste
2 tablespoons finely chopped fresh parsley

Mix all ingredients together in a bowl. Taste and correct seasoning. Let rest to meld flavors.

Serve as a dip or sauce with shrimp, chicken, or simple grilled meats.

RANCH DRESSING

Salad dressings are a mainstay in most kitchens, and they can be costly when purchased already bottled or in packets that need additional ingredients to make them. Many times, along with the high price tag comes a high sodium and fat content. Homemade dressings are a cinch to make, and generally, most of the ingredients are already on hand.

This buttermilk-based dressing is a tasty lowfat alternative to the popular creamy ranch-style dressings. Use the dressing on salads, as sauce, as a dip for chilled vegetables, or as an unusual topping for baked potatoes.

The lowfat buttermilk provides a good backbone for the dressing. Depending on your preference and what you have on hand, the mayonnaise and sour cream are interchangeable. Nonfat plain yogurt gives a slightly tarter taste. The mayonnaise tends to make a slightly thicker dressing. Be sure to taste the dressing and adjust the flavors to your taste.

1 cup lowfat buttermilk
½ cup light *or* nonfat mayonnaise, nonfat sour cream, *or* nonfat plain yogurt, *or* a combination
½ teaspoon Dijon mustard
½ teaspoon Italian herb blend
1 teaspoon sugar
1 small clove garlic, pressed
Dash Worcestershire sauce
Salt and pepper, to taste
1 green top from a scallion, finely chopped, *or* about 1 teaspoon finely chopped onion
1 tablespoon Parmesan cheese, *or* to taste, optional

Put all ingredients in a bowl and mix well. Or use a jar instead: Add ingredients, cover, and shake.

Let dressing rest in refrigerator at least ½ hour to meld flavors. Taste for correct seasoning.

This dressing gets a little stronger as it sits. Keeps about one week in the refrigerator.

MAKES ABOUT 1 CUP

This fast homemade sauce tastes great and uses on-hand ingredients. Use for boiled shrimp (buy them on special or frozen and ready to cook). Leave the shell on: Shrimp stay juicy when cooked in the shell, and they make great finger food—let guests peel them at the table.

1 cup lowfat *or* nonfat mayonnaise *or* sour cream, *or* a mix of the two
3 tablespoons ketchup
3 tablespoons chili sauce
Juice and zest of 1 lemon
1 to 2 tablespoons well-drained horseradish, *or* to taste

½ teaspoon Tabasco sauce
¼ teaspoon Worcestershire sauce

Combine all ingredients in a small bowl, mix well, and refrigerate 2 hours. Serve with grilled seafood and vegetables.

OAT SPICE CAKE

MAKES 80 BITE-SIZE PIECES

This oat spice cake makes a delicious snack or easy dessert. Try it for a party. Cut the cake into small squares so that a bite will be enough to satisfy a sweet tooth (and not add too many calories).

A mixer isn't necessary for the cake, and it can be made in minutes with mostly on-hand ingredients. For added dash, include the zest of a lemon or orange.

1 cup granulated sugar
½ cup brown sugar
2½ cups oats, regular *or* quick-cooking
1 cup unbleached, all-purpose flour
1 stick butter
2 teaspoons ground cinnamon
½ teaspoon ground cloves *or* nutmeg
2 teaspoons baking soda
2 teaspoons vanilla
1 cup raisins *or* chocolate chips
½ cup chopped walnuts, optional
2 eggs, lightly beaten
1 cup nonfat yogurt, buttermilk, or nonfat milk soured with 1 tablespoon vinegar

Preheat oven to 375 degrees F.

Grease a 15 × 10-inch sheet pan.

Put sugars, oats, flour, and butter in a bowl. Rub to coarse crumbs with fingers. Set aside 1 cup crumbs.

Add remaining ingredients and gently mix to incorporate. Pour into prepared pan and spread mixture in pan. Sprinkle top with reserved crumbs.

Bake until cake springs back to touch, about 25 minutes. Cool slightly, and cut into small pieces.

NO-BAKE OAT, PEANUT BUTTER, AND RAISIN NUGGETS

MAKES ABOUT 30

This snack hits the spot with kids and grown-ups alike. These chewy no-bake oat and peanut butter morsels are a cinch to make in the microwave oven with ingredients on hand. Once made, they keep well in an airtight container.

Be sure to use quick-cooking oats. Apple juice works well if orange isn't a favorite. The zest of an orange or lemon gives an additional zap of flavor.

1 cup orange juice
Zest of 1 orange, optional, but good
¼ cup sugar
4 tablespoons crunchy peanut butter
1 teaspoon vanilla
1¾ cups uncooked quick-cooking oats
2 heaping teaspoons cinnamon
Dash salt
½ cup raisins

Put juice, zest (if using), sugar, and peanut butter in a large microwavable bowl. Cover and cook on high 2 minutes. Stir to mix and smooth out any lumps of peanut butter. Add vanilla, oats, cinnamon, salt, and raisins. Mix, then cover and cook on high for 2 more minutes or until liquid is absorbed.

Uncover, mix, and cool slightly. Drop by teaspoonfuls on waxed paper. Gently press each round with a fork to flatten.

Cool in refrigerator. Store in airtight container.

GRANOLA

MAKES ABOUT 9 CUPS

Granola is great for snacking or for breakfast. This granola is easy to make, uses no added fat or sugar, and is flavored by puréed fruit and fruit juice.

8 cups quick-cooking *or* regular oats

Dash salt

1 to 2 tablespoons ground cinnamon, *or* to taste, optional

1 large ripe banana

1 (6-ounce) can *or* ½ to 1 cup apple, pineapple, *or* orange juice (see note below)

1½ tablespoons vanilla

1 tablespoon almond extract, optional

Optional additions

Use about ½ to 1 cup *or* to taste of the following: whole or chopped almonds, walnuts, peanuts, or other nuts; sunflower, pumpkin, or other seeds; shredded coconut, dates, zest of an orange, raisins, or any of your favorites.

Preheat oven to 350 degrees F.

In a bowl, mix oats, salt, and cinnamon with spoon to blend.

In a blender or food processor, process banana, juice, and vanilla and almond extracts until smooth. Add blender ingredients to oats. Add optional ingredients and mix with a spoon. If using raisins, add them after cooking or they will burn and turn hard.

Spread mixture on nonstick or lightly oiled jelly-roll or cookie pan with sides.

Bake at 350 degrees F about 20 minutes, stir once or twice. Then turn oven to 200 degrees F, stir a few times, and bake about 40 minutes or until crisp.

Note: For lumpy granola, use more liquid to clump the oats. For additional sweetness, add a little brown sugar or maple syrup.

ONION DIP

MAKES 1 CUP

Years ago some of my favorite party food included full-fat sour cream mixed with salty dried onion soup dip surrounded by salted potato or corn chips. Salt and fat were fashionable then—now they are considered unstylish. Without the fat or salt, at least in the dip itself, this recipe is a good alternative to that original dip. Be sure to cook the onions slowly so they don't burn.

1 teaspoon vegetable oil
1½ cups finely chopped onion, *or* 1 large onion, finely chopped
3 tablespoons water
Salt and pepper, to taste
Pinch sugar, to taste
Pinch Italian herb blend, *or* your favorite
Dash Worcestershire sauce, to taste
1 cup lowfat *or* nonfat sour cream

Heat oil in medium-size non-stick skillet. Add onions and water, and cook on medium-low heat. Stir occasionally until onions turn golden brown, about 30 minutes.

Toss onions, salt, pepper, sugar, herbs, and Worcestershire sauce into sour cream. Stir and refrigerate up to 1 day or at least 2 hours before serving.

MAKES 16 TO 20 PIECES

An onion tart makes an unusual warm bite-size munchie that's good with beer or white or sparkling wine. Though the pastry dough does have a fair amount of fat in it, the remaining ingredients are practically fat free. The onion mixture can also be served on pita bread (less fat than the puff pastry) or puréed for a room-temperature dip.

Look for whole-grain Dijon mustard because the seeds add texture. The herbs in the onions can be varied, though the pinch of anise or fennel seed gives a nice touch. Make the onions ahead of time, and when ready to cook, roll out the pastry dough, add a slather of Dijon mustard, top with onions, and bake. The tart can be served at room temperature, but is best warm.

1 teaspoon olive oil

4 medium onions, thinly sliced

1 teaspoon sugar

3 sprigs fresh parsley, finely chopped, about 1 tablespoon

¼ teaspoon dried oregano

¼ teaspoon dried rosemary

Pinch dried anise *or* fennel seed, optional, but good

Salt and pepper, to taste

1 sheet frozen puff pastry dough, defrosted according to package instructions

2 tablespoons Dijon mustard, preferably coarse texture

1 tablespoon Parmesan cheese

Preheat oven to 350 degrees F.

Sprinkle a cookie sheet with cornmeal to prevent pastry from sticking.

In a large sauté pan, heat oil and add onions, sugar, herbs, salt, and pepper. Stir, then cover and cook on medium-low heat for about 20 minutes. Stir occasionally so onions don't burn. They will cook in their own juice and become soft and almost creamy in texture. Remove from heat.

Roll out pastry to a 10 × 14-inch rectangle. Roll edges up

about ½ inch to make border. Place on prepared cookie sheet. Spread mustard on the pastry and then the onions. Sprinkle with Parmesan cheese and bake for 15 to 20 minutes or until top and crust is golden.

Cut into small squares to serve.

QUICK ONION SAUTÉ

SERVES 4

When I tire of the usual selection of vegetables, I cook onions for an economical, versatile, and satisfying vegetable dish. Fresh onions—red, white, yellow, or green—are always on hand in my kitchen, usually to flavor other foods. When cooked alone onions are a delicious side dish with grilled meats and poultry, a tasty topping for pizza, or a simple spread for garlic toast.

Mix and match your onions depending on what you have on hand. If using the mixture for crackers or toast to serve as a nibble with drinks, top with a small dollop of non- or lowfat sour cream and a sprinkle of finely chopped green onion or grated Parmesan cheese.

Onions have a fairly high water content, so it's not necessary to add liquid, though do cook them on medium-low heat so they don't burn. A touch of vinegar as the mixture cooks rounds out the flavors. Be sure to taste as the mixture cooks to adjust the seasonings to your preference.

1 tablespoon olive *or* vegetable oil

5 medium onions, mixed yellow, red, white, *or* any combination, peeled and thinly sliced

2 cloves garlic, pressed

½ teaspoon mustard, *or* to taste

2 teaspoons Worcestershire sauce, *or* to taste

½ teaspoon Italian herb blend, *or* to taste

Salt and pepper, to taste

1 teaspoon vinegar, *or* to taste

2 medium green onions, finely chopped

1 heaping tablespoon grated Parmesan cheese, optional

Heat oil in large skillet. Add onions, garlic, mustard, Worcestershire sauce, herbs, salt, and pepper. Cook on medium-low heat, stirring often, until onions are soft and golden, about 15 minutes.

Add vinegar, stir, and taste for correct seasoning.

Serve sprinkled with green onions and cheese (if using).

TO CHEW ON

I live on good soup, not fine words.

—Molière

GRILLED ONION SALAD

SERVES 4 TO 6

Expand this basic salad and use other seasonal vegetables—try bell peppers, zucchini, or tomatoes, to name a few. Think about color and crunch when adding other vegetables. Cook the vegetables the same way as the onions—cut in half—on the grill or under the broiler.

The exact proportions for the herbs, vinegar, and oil are variable depending on your taste and the sweetness of the onions. Simply dress the onions with a few tablespoons of balsamic, rice, or wine vinegar. Or, use the orange juice–based recipe below.

4 medium onions, preferably sweet, spring, or red onions
2 tablespoons olive oil, for cooking
1 to 2 tablespoons fresh chopped herbs such as parsley, basil, chervil, thyme, *or* 1 to 2 teaspoons dried mixed herbs, to taste
Salt and pepper, to taste
¼ cup orange juice
1 small clove garlic, pressed

Rinse the onions, but do not peel them. Cut in half through the diameter of each onion. Brush with olive oil. Lay cut side up if broiling, or cut side down if grilling over medium-heated coals.

Cook until tops are browned and flesh soft. If necessary, remove onions, cut off cooked part, brush newly cut side with olive oil, and continue cooking.

Put cooked onions into a bowl. Add herbs, salt, pepper, orange juice, and garlic. Taste for correct seasoning. Serve warm or at room temperature.

SERVES 8

Make these easy drop shortcake biscuits a year-round dessert. The biscuits keep well and won't get soggy with the juices from sliced fresh summer fruits such as peaches, nectarines, or berries.

2 cups unbleached, all-purpose flour
1½ tablespoons sugar
¼ heaping teaspoon ground cinnamon
Dash salt
1 teaspoon baking powder
½ teaspoon baking soda
4 tablespoons butter, softened
1 scant cup orange juice
Zest of 1 orange, about 1 heaping tablespoon

Preheat oven to 425 degrees F.

Put flour, sugar, cinnamon, salt, baking powder, and baking soda in a mixing bowl. Mix with a fork.

Add butter in small pieces and mix with fork or fingers to incorporate with flour.

Add juice and zest. Mix to incorporate. If dough is very sticky, sprinkle about 1 tablespoon flour on it and knead for about half a minute in bowl. Dough should be slightly sticky.

Drop heaping tablespoonfuls of dough on ungreased baking sheet. Gently spread to about 4 inches wide and 1 inch thick.

Bake for 8 to 10 minutes or until lightly browned on top. Cool on wire rack.

To serve, gently slice horizontally, put fruit on bottom half, top, and add more fruit and whipped cream or a little ice cream.

VERMICELLI SALAD

For a change of pace this is a white salad rather than a typical green one. The main ingredient can be spaghetti, angel hair pasta, or cooked rice noodles. Asian mung bean thread vermicelli (also called cellophane noodles) are another possibility. These noodles become soft, slippery, and translucent when cooked and have a slightly chewy texture. They don't have much of a distinct flavor of their own and take well to the bold flavors of the dressing. Look for them in the Asian food section of well-stocked supermarkets.

Vegetables add texture to the soft noodles. Add your favorites. The dressing is a bold combination of fresh garlic and ginger with an undertone of sesame oil.

6 ounces spaghetti *or* vermicelli, cooked and drained, (see note below)

2 carrots, shredded

4 green onions, finely chopped

¼ small head cabbage, finely shredded

1 cup fresh bean sprouts, optional

1 tablespoon chopped fresh cilantro

2 tablespoons sesame seeds *or* chopped peanuts

In a large serving bowl, toss all ingredients except cilantro, and seeds or nuts.

Dressing

1 large clove garlic, pressed

1 piece pickled ginger, *or* 1 slice fresh ginger, finely chopped, about 1 teaspoon

2 teaspoons Asian sesame oil

Zest and juice of 1 large orange *or* lemon

1 or 2 teaspoons rice *or* white vinegar

1 teaspoon light soy sauce, *or* to taste

Pinch sugar

Combine ingredients and taste to correct seasoning. Toss on noodles and taste again for correct seasoning. Serve sprinkled with cilantro and seeds or nuts.

Note: To cook Asian vermicelli, bring a large pot of water to boil. Add vermicelli and cook for about 3 minutes or until it is soft and translucent. Drain in a strainer, rinse under cold water, and drain.

ZITI À LA CAFÉ MADDALENA

Opposite the train station in the tiny town of Dunsmuir, California, sits the tiny Café Maddalena. There, owner-chef Maddalena Serra dishes up the best Sardinian/Italian food north of Sacramento. This fast, zesty, and easy-to-prepare dish is served at the restaurant. Maddalena created the recipe with on-hand ingredients in a friend's kitchen during a recent trip to Italy. Serve the pasta as a starter course or double it for a main course to serve 4 to 6.

Ziti are thin tubes of dried pasta, easily available at the supermarket. Bold and robust flavors are a mainstay of the dish, and some of the ingredients, particularly the olives and anchovies, are salty. Taste varies with the brand used, so adjust the flavors to your preference. Look for kalamata type olives in the deli department. Black canned olives will work, but try to add some green ones also. Cannellini beans, known also as white kidney beans, are available canned and dried. If cannellini beans can't be found, use Great Northern beans.

1 tablespoon olive oil

½ cup cooked cannellini beans

3 tablespoons chopped assorted olives, about 10 olives

4 tablespoons chopped fresh parsley, Italian flat leaf preferred

¼ medium white *or* red onion, finely chopped

2 to 3 large cloves garlic, finely chopped

1 or 2 anchovies, rinsed and chopped, optional, but good

Dash red pepper flakes, optional

Salt and pepper, to taste

1 cup chopped canned *or* fresh tomatoes (peeled, if fresh, about 4 Roma tomatoes)

½ pound ziti pasta, cooked al dente, drained, reserve ½ cup cooking liquid

Heat oil in large skillet. Add all ingredients except tomatoes and pasta. Cook on medium-high heat, stirring occasionally, until onion just begins to soften and becomes translucent, about 2 or 3 minutes. Add tomatoes with juice and a few tablespoons reserved pasta water and cook on high heat, stirring, for about 1 minute. Taste for correct seasoning.

Add pasta and a few more tablespoons water if mixture is dry. Cook on medium-high to heat through.

Serve immediately sprinkled with freshly grated Parmesan cheese, if desired.

CHOW MEIN WITH OYSTER SAUCE

SERVES 4

In Chinese culture, noodles symbolize a long life and are frequently part of birthday and holiday meals. This easy noodle (chow mein) dish is from Sacramento's David SooHoo, owner-chef of SooHoo's. The dish is high in taste, texture, and color, while low in price and fat.

Use the sauce to flavor chicken, shrimp, vegetables, or rice. Create your own dish with other such vegetables as broccoli, bean sprouts, or green onion, or use about ½ pound raw chicken or meat cut in bite-size pieces. Stir-fry meat before vegetables. Mushrooms and snow peas run about $3 a pound, but they don't weigh much, and you only need a few pieces of each. Both can be thinly sliced to go further. Look for fresh Chinese egg noodles in the produce section of the supermarket or use spaghetti or fresh pasta noodles.

Sauce

1 tablespoon oyster sauce (available in Asian section of supermarket)

1 scant cup low-sodium, low-fat chicken broth *or* water

Pinch salt, *or* to taste

Pinch pepper, *or* to taste

1 teaspoon sugar

2 tablespoons cornstarch

Mix all ingredients in a small bowl. Set aside.

Chow Mein

1 (16-ounce) package fresh Chinese egg noodles or spaghetti, cooked according to package instructions, rinsed with cold water, drained, and kept warm

1 tablespoon vegetable oil

1 medium yellow onion, thinly sliced

1 medium carrot, cut in ½-inch-long matchsticks

8 medium mushrooms, thinly sliced

1 cup water *or* broth

10 snow peas, strung and cut into lengthwise slivers

2 medium green onions, finely chopped, optional, for garnish

Few sprigs cilantro, optional for garnish

In a nonstick or lightly oiled large skillet, spread noodles and cook on medium-low heat until brown and crunchy. Turn noodles and cook on other side. Do this while stir-frying vegetables.

In wok or heavy skillet, heat oil on high until it just begins to smoke. Add onion, carrot, and mushrooms and stir-fry about 30 seconds. Add liquid, cover, and cook about 1 minute. Add peas and sauce. Toss and cook until sauce thickens, about 30 seconds. Cover and keep warm as you finish cooking noodles.

To serve, put noodles on a platter, top with vegetable mixture and a sprinkling, if desired, of green onions and cilantro.

MAKES ABOUT 5 CUPS

Colorful and tasty, this summer salad mixes soft pasta with crunchy cabbage. It's easy and can be made ahead for picnics and parties. Cabbage and pasta are low-cost foods that make quick and healthy meals. Try the salad as part of a vegetarian meal or as a zippy side dish for grilled fish, chicken, or meat.

Any pasta will work, just cook it according to the directions on the package. I like the flavor of fresh Chinese noodles (the kind you find in chow mein, not the crunchy ones from a can), and the noodles cook in two or three minutes. Look for the fresh noodles in the produce section of the supermarket. After draining the pasta, toss with a teaspoon or two of olive oil to keep it from sticking.

Because I don't like my salad dripping in dressing, this tangy one with celery seed and mustard just coats the cabbage and pasta. A fruity olive oil lets you use less oil while retaining the olive oil flavor. Use your favorite oil and vinegar dressing if you wish. For added color, shred a little carrot to sprinkle on top of the salad.

⅓ medium head red cabbage, finely shredded

½ pound fresh Chinese noodles *or* your favorite pasta, cooked, drained, and tossed with 1 teaspoon olive oil

3 green onions, finely chopped

Dressing

3 tablespoons wine *or* cider vinegar, *or* to taste

1 tablespoon lemon juice, *or* to taste

2 teaspoons olive oil, *or* to taste

½ teaspoon celery seed

½ teaspoon Dijon *or* dry mustard

Salt and pepper, to taste

Pinch sugar, to taste, optional

Mix dressing ingredients and toss with salad ingredients. Taste for correct seasoning.

Chill. Taste before serving. Many times the pasta soaks up the dressing and so the flavors need to be adjusted.

LAST-MINUTE SUMMER PASTA SALAD

SERVES 4 TO 5

Here's a delicious summertime dish that needs only cooked pasta and lots of fresh raw vegetables to create a colorful, meal-in-one salad. This garden-fresh creation uses the bumper crops of such summer favorites as tomatoes, cucumbers, zucchini, onions, and green bell peppers. Try the salad for a Labor Day party or picnic.

If desired, cook and drain the pasta and add the vegetables for a warm-cold effect. Or, make the salad in the morning and serve it cold. Don't worry about exact proportions, the salad is forgiving and adjustable to personal taste. Some optional additions include green onions, radishes, olives, drained marinated artichoke hearts, green beans, and corn. Shred a little cooked fish, meat, or poultry on the salad, if desired. Dress the pasta with your favorite dressing, or use this very simple one with a few fresh herbs with a little olive oil and lemon juice and garlic.

4 cups cooked pasta, *or* about ½ pound dry pasta cooked according to instructions on package

2 medium tomatoes, seeded, if desired, and chopped

1 medium cucumber, peeled, cut lengthwise, seeded, and sliced

½ small red onion, *or* to taste, thinly sliced

½ green bell pepper, finely chopped

1 small yellow *or* green zucchini, coarsely shredded

1 carrot, sliced into thin ribbons with a vegetable peeler

Toss all ingredients in a large bowl with dressing (see recipe below). Taste for correct seasoning. Serve warm with just-cooked pasta and cold vegetables, or cold.

Dressing

Small handful fresh basil leaves *or* other fresh herb (thyme, oregano, *or* a mix) torn into small pieces

3 sprigs fresh parsley, finely chopped
1 medium-large clove garlic, pressed
1 to 2 tablespoons fruity olive oil, *or* to taste
Juice and zest of 1 lemon *or* about 4 tablespoons wine vinegar, *or* to taste
Salt and pepper, to taste
1 teaspoon capers, *or* to taste, coarsely chopped

Put all ingredients in a small jar. Cover jar and shake vigorously to incorporate.

SERVES 6

Make this fast dish with ingredients right from the cupboard. Frying the pasta before adding the tomatoes adds another layer of flavor to the dish. A variation of this pasta dish originated in the early thirteenth century with the Spanish Jews.

Expand the dish to your taste as I did: Never one to turn down garlic, I like to press a clove into the simmering pasta. Further embellishments include a pinch of dried herbs or some chopped fresh basil, oregano, or parsley. To let the flavors meld, make this dish a day ahead and reheat before serving. Serve it alone or with almost any chicken dish and a salad.

1 to 2 tablespoons olive oil
1 (12-ounce) package small shaped pasta (shells, butterflies, etc.)
1 (15-ounce) can stewed tomatoes
3 cups water
Salt and pepper, to taste
Pinch of sugar, if desired, depending on acidity of tomatoes

Put oil in a large saucepan and heat on medium. Add pasta and pan-fry until golden brown, stirring so pieces don't overbrown.

Add tomatoes, water, salt, and pepper. Bring to a boil, turn to simmer, and cook semicovered, for about 10 minutes. Stir occasionally to keep pasta from sticking. Taste, correct seasoning, and add sugar, if desired. Cook until pasta is tender and liquid is absorbed.

Remove from heat and let sit, covered, about 10 minutes. Before serving, stir again. If reheating, be sure to cover and use low heat. Serve with Parmesan cheese on the side.

PRIZE-WINNING PEACH COBBLER

SERVES 8

This recipe took first place at the Sacramento Certified Farmers' Market Peach Cobbler Contest. Elizabeth Keown, a young eighty-three years old, made her prize cobbler from a recipe adapted from an age-old favorite she cut from a 1949 newspaper.

Peaches are a great summer buy at farmers' markets or in supermarkets. In winter, use frozen peaches. This recipe is a winner for me because the peaches are simply flavored and the topping is small cinnamon spirals, rather than the usual crumb topping.

6 cups fresh peeled, sliced peaches, about 6 large peaches
1 cup sugar
2 tablespoons lemon juice
1 teaspoon almond extract
2 cups unbleached, all-purpose flour
2½ teaspoons baking powder
¼ teaspoon salt
2 tablespoons sugar
6 tablespoons butter
1 egg, beaten
⅓ cup lowfat milk
½ cup sugar mixed with ¼ teaspoon ground cinnamon *or* to taste

Preheat oven to 400 degrees F.

Put peaches in buttered 10 × 10-inch baking dish. Combine 1 cup sugar, lemon juice, and almond extract, and sprinkle over peaches.

Sift flour, baking powder, salt, and 2 tablespoons sugar into a bowl. Cut in butter.

Combine egg and milk. Stir into flour mixture. If dough is dry, add extra milk, 1 teaspoon at a time, until the dough reaches the right consistency to roll out.

On a lightly floured board, roll dough into a 8 × 10-inch rectangle. Sprinkle with cinnamon and sugar mixture. Roll up in jelly-roll fashion. Cut in ½-inch sections.

Place sections spiral side up on top of peaches. Bake 25 to 30 minutes.

POACHED PEARS

SERVES 8 (½ PEAR EACH)

Homey or elegant, poached pears are a classic and simple dessert. This recipe is simple and offers many ways to flavor the fruit.

Poaching means simmering in liquid. These pears work well with fruit juice, water, wine, or a combination. The liquid can be flavored with cinnamon, ginger, vanilla, or orange, to name a few options. Look for unblemished, barely ripe fruit; Boscs and Bartletts hold their shape best during cooking.

If pears aren't available, try poaching peaches, apples, or nectarines, or a medley. If wine is not available, use orange juice or apple juice. The idea is to briefly cook the fruit so it is soft, not mushy. Generally, 6 tablespoons of sugar to 1 cup of liquid works well, though I've used less because I don't like overly sweet fruit. My friend, Elaine Corn, recently poached her pears in Zinfandel wine and star anise (a licorice-tasting spice)—a yummy combination.

Serve the fruit in a small bowl with some of the cooking liquid and a sprinkle of zest or, if desired, dress it up with a dollop of whipped cream or ice cream or even a drizzle of chocolate sauce.

1 cup water and 1 cup red wine *or* apple *or* orange juice

½ teaspoon ground cinnamon, *or* 1 stick whole

½ inch fresh ginger, crushed, *or* ¼ teaspoon dried, *or* ¼ teaspoon ground cloves

6 tablespoons sugar, *or* to taste

4 pears, peeled and cut in half with seeds removed

Zest of ½ orange, finely chopped, optional, for garnish

In a large saucepan, bring all ingredients except pears and orange zest to a boil.

Add pears, reduce heat, cover, and gently simmer for 5 to 10 minutes, or until pears are just soft. Cooking time may be a little longer depending on the pear.

Serve warm or at room temperature with some of the sauce and a tiny sprinkle of zest, if using, and a simple cookie or cake.

PEAR AND ORANGE CHUTNEY

SERVES 4 TO 5 AS A SIDE DISH

Chutneys add pizzazz as accompaniments for roasted and grilled meats and poultry. These cooked and colorful combinations vary depending on the fruits in season and how sweet or pungent you choose to make the dish.

Mostly fruit chutneys (vegetables also work) are a good way to use very ripe (not rotten) produce. Other fruit-vegetable combinations (the number is almost countless) include tomato-onion and corn-raisin. Other fruits that work well include plums, raisins, peaches, pineapple, mangoes, and apples.

The constant flavor elements in chutney are sweet and sour—how much of each depends on your taste and the fruits used. Cinnamon gives a sweet undertone, while an equal amount of mustard seed adds a touch of spice and heat. I like cider vinegar for a mellower flavor. The idea is to balance the flavors so that no ingredient overpowers another.

2 pears, cored and chopped
1 small onion, finely chopped
Zest, juice, and flesh of 1 orange
1 small piece fresh ginger, finely chopped
⅓ cup raisins
1 to 2 tablespoons sugar, *or* to taste
⅓ cup cider vinegar, *or* to taste
⅓ cup water *or* orange juice
½ teaspoon ground cinnamon
½ teaspoon mustard seeds, optional
Pinch red pepper flakes, *or* to taste, optional

Put all ingredients in a saucepan. Bring to a boil, cover, and simmer on medium-low heat for 15 to 20 minutes or until fruit is soft. Taste for correct seasoning. Cool and serve at room temperature.

STEWED PEAR SAUCE

MAKES 3 TO 4 CUPS

Here's a variation on applesauce that uses pears instead of the traditional apples. Don't worry about exact measurements—they may vary depending on the sweetness and size of the fruit. Make as little or as much as you have pears on hand. Serve the sauce alone, with cookies, or as a topping for Angel Food Cake or Pumpkin Spice Cake (pages 130 and 213).

10 pears, peeled, cored, and chopped

¼ cup sugar, or to taste

½ teaspoon ground cinnamon

¼ teaspoon ground ginger, *or* to taste, optional

1 teaspoon vanilla

1½ cups apple *or* orange juice

Zest of orange *or* lemon

Toss all ingredients into a large saucepan. Bring to a boil, cover, and simmer for 10 to 15 minutes or until fruit is soft but not mushy. More liquid can be added for more sauce.

PEA SOUP IN A PINCH

MAKES 4 CUPS

When green peas are fresh, I can never get enough of them. No matter how many pounds I buy, most are eaten before they reach the cooking pot. When fresh peas aren't available, frozen peas are a must to have on hand for last-minute additions to casseroles, pastas, and rice. Use them for a delicious, low-cost quick soup any time of the year.

In this recipe, a few tablespoons of raw rice are added to thicken the soup. Use chicken broth for a richer flavor. Consider adding your favorite herbs or try curry, thyme, ginger, or cumin for a change of pace.

1 to 3 teaspoons olive oil
1 medium onion, chopped
2 cups frozen peas
2 tablespoons uncooked rice
½ teaspoon dried dill *or* basil *or* your favorite herb, *or* to taste
Salt and pepper, to taste
4 cups water, chicken broth, *or* a mix
¼ cup nonfat yogurt *or* sour cream, for garnish

In a large saucepan, heat olive oil and add onion. Sauté for a few minutes or until onion begins to soften.

Add remaining ingredients, except for yogurt, cover, and cook about 15 minutes or until rice is soft.

Purée mixture in a blender or food processor, if desired. Taste for correct seasoning. Serve hot with a dollop of yogurt or sour cream. Sprinkle yogurt with a dash of paprika, if desired.

EASY SPLIT PEA SOUP

MAKES ABOUT 8 CUPS

Split peas and lentils are two legumes that do not need to be soaked before cooking. They cook quickly, and can be served as a side dish to meats and poultry. I've always had an addictive desire for this soup. My mother made it often and it is very satisfying on a cold winter night.

1 tablespoon olive oil
1 large onion, chopped
3 cloves garlic, chopped
2 large carrots, chopped
1 stalk celery, chopped
2 cups dried split peas, picked over and rinsed
1 bay leaf
Large pinch dried thyme
1 meaty ham hock, *or* other smoked meat such as turkey *or* 1 smoked sausage, whole
8 cups water
Salt and pepper, to taste, depending on meat used

In a large pot, heat olive oil and add onion, garlic, carrots, and celery. Sauté until vegetables begin to soften or sweat. Add remaining ingredients. Bring to a boil for 1 or 2 minutes, then turn to simmer, cover, and cook about 45 minutes to 1 hour or until peas are soft.

Remove ham hock, if using, or meat and cut into small pieces. Remove bay leaf.

Purée in a food processor or food mill, if desired, or leave soup chunky. Serve with croutons or a loaf of crusty bread and a salad.

PIPERADE

Piperade is a classic Basque dish of ripe tomatoes, onions, and peppers that jazzes up everything from scrambled eggs to grilled fish, poultry, and meat. It's also delicious spread on toast as a munchie with drinks.

This dish is colorful, lowfat, and makes good use of low-cost summer vegetables and fresh basil. The vegetable juice, particularly that of the tomatoes, allows for the mixture to cook on low heat without burning. I peel the tomatoes, though it's not necessary.

½ to 1 tablespoon fruity olive oil
2 cloves garlic, pressed *or* minced
2 small onions, chopped
3 large tomatoes, chopped, including juice
1 medium green *or* red bell pepper, cut in ¼-inch pieces
1 tablespoon red wine vinegar
2 tablespoons minced fresh basil (about 8 leaves)
Salt and pepper, to taste

Heat oil in large pan. Add garlic and onions. Sauté on medium-high heat about 5 minutes until onions begin to soften.

Add remaining ingredients, cover, and cook on low heat for 10 minutes stirring occasionally. Remove cover, and continue cooking on low until vegetables are soft and well blended, about 20 minutes. Taste to adjust seasoning.

If desired, scramble eggs into the mixture. Or, use as a bed for poached eggs, grilled fish, meat, or poultry.

PORK AND VEGETABLE STEW

Stews are an economical and easy way to cook inexpensive pork, lamb, or beef cuts such as butt, loin, shoulder, or chuck. Generally these cuts take well to slow cooking because this method makes the meat tender. Perfect for cold winter meals, stews can be made ahead and frozen.

Pork butt or loin roasts are usually about two pounds. Cut the roast in half to use one pound for stew and the remainder to marinate and grill, or make the entire recipe as a stew to serve at least eight. To stretch your meat, add other root vegetables, including turnips and parsnips.

3 to 4 tablespoons unbleached, all-purpose flour

Salt and pepper, to taste

2 pounds boneless pork butt, fat removed, cut into 1-inch cubes

2 tablespoons vegetable *or* olive oil

2 large cloves garlic, pressed

2 large onions, peeled and cut into eighths

4 stalks celery, cut into 1-inch chunks

4 large carrots, scraped and cut into 1-inch rounds

4 tablespoons finely chopped fresh parsley

1 heaping teaspoon dried herb such as oregano, cumin, sage, *or* your favorite blend

1 bay leaf

1 can beer *or* about 1 cup red wine, chicken stock, *or* water

2 cups water

8 medium potatoes, peeled and cut into small chunks

Splash of vinegar, *or* to taste, optional

In a bowl, mix flour, salt, and pepper. Toss meat in flour to lightly coat.

Heat oil in large pot, add meat, and stir and brown on medium-high heat. Drain if

(Continued)

there is a lot of fat. Lower heat, add garlic and onion, and sauté a few minutes.

Add celery, carrots, half the parsley, herbs, and liquids. Bring to a boil, cover, and simmer about 45 minutes. Add potatoes and continue cooking until meat is tender and potatoes are cooked, about 15 to 20 minutes.

Taste for correct seasoning, add a splash of vinegar if desired. Serve with remaining 2 tablespoons of parsley sprinkled on top.

Potatoes are one of the most versatile foods available. Wholesome, inexpensive, and filled with complex carbohydrates, protein, vitamins, and minerals, they make the ultimate fast food—especially when cooked in the microwave oven.

Russets make the best baked potatoes. To bake raw potatoes: Preheat oven to 400 degrees F. Scrub potatoes well. Trim the ends off. Don't wrap in aluminum foil as they will steam, rather than bake. Bake for 40 to 60 minutes, depending on the size of the potato. Prick the potato with a fork at least once, about halfway through cooking, if desired, to release steam and make the flesh flaky. Potato is done when it is soft when pushed with fingers.

To microwave a raw potato: Prick potato once or twice with a fork so it won't burst as it cooks. Cook in microwave oven according to the manufacturer's instructions, usually about 7 minutes on high for a medium potato.

TO CHEW ON

2 ounces of potato chips (about 30) have 300 calories and 20 grams of fat while a baked 7-ounce (nearly ½ pound) potato has 220 calories with no fat grams. Convenience potatoes—dried, frozen, scalloped, creamed—are high in sodium, fat, and additives. It's your choice.

SMASHED POTATOES WITH ITALIAN STIR-FRY

SERVES 4

Smashed potatoes are almost mashed potatoes that make an unusual bed for stir-fries. Use red, white, or russet potatoes. Reds and whites hold their shape better. Save time and don't peel the potatoes; the skins give added texture and flavor.

An Italian stir-fry! Why not! The quick and simple stir-fry cooking technique isn't only for Asian food. This easy and versatile dish makes improvisation a cinch—use favorite seasonal vegetables and fresh or dried herbs. Look for Italian blend seasoning in the herb and spice section of the supermarket or make your own mixture of oregano, basil, or rosemary. Be sure to cut vegetables into bite-size pieces so they will cook quickly.

Smashed potatoes

1 pound potatoes, unpeeled, cut in chunks and boiled until tender, not mushy, and drained
Salt and pepper, to taste
Drizzle of fruity olive oil, about 1 or 2 teaspoons, or to taste

Place potatoes on serving platter, and with a fork, smash them three or four times to make a bed for the vegetables. Season with salt and pepper, and drizzle the olive oil over the potatoes. Immediately top with vegetables and serve.

Italian Stir-Fry

1 to 3 teaspoons olive oil
1 medium onion, thinly sliced
1 large clove garlic, minced
½ green or red bell pepper, thinly sliced
1 pound seasonal vegetable of choice such as broccoli, zucchini, green beans, cut into bite-size pieces
½ pound boneless chicken, turkey, or meat of choice, cut in small pieces, or use ground, optional
1 teaspoon Italian herb blend, or to taste
Salt and pepper, to taste

1 tablespoon fresh minced
   parsley, optional, as garnish
Grated Parmesan cheese,
      served on the side as
      garnish

Heat a large skillet with the oil and add the onion and garlic. Cook on medium-high heat until the onion begins to soften. Add bell peppers and vegetables and stir-fry for 1 or 2 minutes, until vegetables just begin to soften. Add meat (if using), and herbs, salt, and pepper, and continue to stir-fry until meat is cooked and vegetables are slightly crunchy.

Taste and correct seasoning. Serve over smashed potatoes and top with parsley if desired. Serve grated Parmesan cheese on the side.

MARCIE'S RESTUFFED BAKED POTATOES

MAKES 4 POTATOES

Nothing satisfies more than a baked potato served plain with salt and pepper or embellished with all the usual fatty suspects—butter, sour cream, olive oil, or margarine. (Look for the low- or nonfat versions of sour cream, yogurt, and mayonnaise; these are just as tasty without all the fat). To cut time, microwave the potatoes first, then reheat in oven.

For a more unusual treatment, bake then stuff the potato with a purée of any of your favorite vegetables such as drained marinated artichoke hearts, broccoli, carrots, red bell peppers, or sun-dried tomatoes, to name a few. Salsa, garlic, curry powder, or fresh herbs such as basil, dill, and parsley also make tasty flavor enhancers for the potato.

4 large baked potatoes, flesh removed to a bowl, skins saved

¼ cup nonfat *or* lowfat milk, *or* enough to moisten potato

1 (6-ounce) jar marinated artichoke hearts, drained and finely chopped, *or* 1 cup cooked favorite vegetable, finely chopped

1 tablespoon parsley, finely chopped, optional

1 large clove garlic, pressed

Salt and pepper, to taste

4 tablespoons grated Parmesan cheese, optional

Preheat oven to 400 degrees F.

Mix all ingredients, except potato skins and cheese, in a bowl. Taste for correct seasoning. Stuff into the potato skins. Sprinkle with cheese, 1 tablespoon per potato, if using. Bake about 10 minutes or until tops are golden.

CREAMY POTATOES (WITHOUT THE CREAM)

MAKES 4 TO 5 CUPS

The creamy texture of this dish comes from shredded potatoes cooked as hot liquid is added slowly and the mixture is stirred. As the liquid evaporates, more is added until the potatoes cook to a creamy consistency. This makes a nice winter dish, good with roasted meats or poultry or as a vegetarian entrée. For variation, add finely chopped vegetables or herbs. Figure one medium-size potato per person; this dish can be halved easily to serve two or three people.

1 tablespoon olive oil

1 medium onion, finely chopped

2 cloves garlic, pressed

2 pounds russet potatoes (about 4 good size), peeled and coarsely shredded, gently squeezed of excess liquid

Salt and pepper, to taste

1 heaping teaspoon dried herbs *or* 1 tablespoon fresh such as basil, oregano, *or* thyme, optional

2 to 3 cups chicken broth, water, *or* a mixture, simmering

2 tablespoons finely chopped fresh parsley

½ cup peas *or* corn, optional

1 small piece bacon, cooked and crumbled, optional

4 tablespoons grated Parmesan cheese

In a large saucepan, heat olive oil and sauté onion on medium heat until it just begins to soften. Add garlic, potatoes, salt, pepper, and herbs (if using). Mix and add a cup of liquid. Cook on medium heat. Stir often so potatoes absorb almost all the liquid. Add another ½ to 1 cup liquid and a tablespoon of parsley. Stir and continue cooking, adding more liquid if necessary, until the potatoes are soft and creamy, about 15 to 20 minutes.

As potatoes finish cooking, add peas, corn, or bacon (if using). When potatoes are done, stir in cheese, adjust seasoning, and serve sprinkled with remaining 1 tablespoon parsley.

MARCIE'S MASHED POTATOES

SERVES 4

For comfort food, I turn to mashed potatoes. As a healthy fast food, potatoes cook in minutes particularly if cut in chunks for mashing. Save more time and leave the skins on for added texture, flavor, and nutrients.

The variations for mashed potatoes are almost endless. I stumbled on a favorite when I realized I had no milk and had just drained all the cooking water from the pot. I opened the refrigerator and found that I did have lowfat sour cream. A large dollop mixed into the potatoes along with salt and pepper made them a hit at dinner.

Note: *Any kind of potato will do for mashed potatoes. Russets have a low moisture and high starch content and the dry flesh makes fluffy mashed potatoes. Red and white potatoes have high moisture and low starch. They stay firm for salads and don't fall apart easily.*

4 medium potatoes, scrubbed and chunked

Water to cover potatoes

Few shakes salt

Some Optional Cooking Additions

4 to 6 large cloves garlic, peeled

Handful of fresh chopped herb such as parsley

2 or 3 green onions, finely chopped

Some Optional Mashing Additions

½ cup cooking water, *or* to taste

½ cup low- *or* nonfat milk, *or* to taste

½ cup low- *or* nonfat sour cream, *or* to taste

In a large pot, put potatoes, water, salt, and any one of the optional cooking ingredients (if using). Bring to a boil, cover, and turn to medium-high heat. Cook until potatoes are soft when pierced with a fork, about 10 minutes. Drain and save cooking liquid if using to mash potatoes. Leave top off pot so potatoes will dry out a bit.

Mash with a fork or potato masher; using a blender or food processor makes the potatoes very gluey.

Add one or more of optional mashing additions adjusting the amount to get desired consistency and taste. Let your guests add salt, pepper, and butter, if desired.

POTATO AND SLAW SALAD

SERVES 4 TO 6

Combine two favorite salads—potato and coleslaw—with a refreshing celery seed dressing. Rather than the typical heavy mayonnaise base (it doesn't hold up without refrigeration), this dressing uses cider vinegar with a dash of olive oil for flavor. Of course, your favorite mayonnaise or oil-and-vinegar dressing will also work.

The soft potatoes and crunchy cabbage add an unusual texture to this colorful, flavorful salad. Enjoy it with grilled hamburgers or chicken any time of the year.

Red potatoes make good salads because they hold their shape and have a slightly creamy texture. Russets will work, just don't overcook them. Cider vinegar gives a mellow flavor, or use any good white wine vinegar. A little fruity olive oil goes a long way in flavor and a short way in fat calories. A few pieces of orange or lemon zest (the outer portion of the peel) make a nice addition to the dressing. Adjust the flavors according to your taste just before serving.

1 small clove garlic, pressed
1 teaspoon mustard, *or* to taste
1 teaspoon celery seed
Salt and pepper, to taste
6 tablespoons cider vinegar
2 teaspoons olive oil, *or* to taste
Zest of ½ orange, optional
2 pounds red potatoes, boiled, cooled, peeled (if desired), and diced

½ medium head red *or* green cabbage, finely shredded
4 green onions *or* ¼ medium red onion, finely chopped
1 small carrot, shredded, optional

For the dressing, combine garlic, mustard, celery seed, salt, pepper, vinegar, olive oil, and zest (if using) in a small bowl. Stir and let rest as remaining ingredients are prepared.

Put potatoes, cabbage, onion, and carrot (if using) in a large serving bowl. Toss with dressing and taste for correct seasoning.

POTATO DUMPLINGS

MAKES 40 TO 44 (1-INCH) DUMPLINGS

These light dumplings (similar to Italian gnocchi) use old russet potatoes and take just minutes to prepare if you use a microwave oven to cook the potatoes for 7 to 10 minutes. The dish is practically fat free when tossed with a tomato sauce. Other sauces such as pesto, fontina cheese, or cream are delicious also, but higher in fat.

Variables such as the age of the potatoes and weather (humid or dry) may affect the amount of flour used. Use old russet potatoes and bake them with an incision to allow steam to escape. Add only enough flour to bind and make a barely sticky dough. Don't overknead or the dumplings will be heavy. Cook them in lots of boiling water. Don't freeze them or they'll be mushy when cooked.

4 medium potatoes (about 2 pounds), baked, slightly cooled, and peeled
½ teaspoon salt *or* to taste
1 to 2 cups unbleached, all-purpose flour
Few sprigs fresh parsley, finely chopped, about 1 tablespoon, optional
½ teaspoon dried basil *or* oregano, optional

Mash the potatoes with a fork or put them through a food mill or potato ricer. Add salt, about ⅓ cup flour, and remaining ingredients (if using).

Mix with hands until dough begins to stick together.

Transfer dough to wooden board and knead lightly, adding only enough flour to keep dough from sticking to board and hands. The dough should take no more than 4 to 5 minutes to make and is ready when it is soft, pliable, and slightly sticky. Don't overwork the dough.

Divide the dough into orange-size balls. Lightly flour your hands, and roll each piece into a long roll about the thickness of your thumb. Cut rolls into 1-inch pieces.

Cook dumplings in a large pot of boiling salted water. Drain and toss with sauce.

To store for a short time, place the dumplings on a lightly floured plate or baking sheet, and store overnight uncovered in the refrigerator.

SERVES 6 TO 8

The chill of fall days makes me think of the warmth and comfort of hearty soups. These are great make-ahead-and-reheat meals-in-one. Potato soups are very versatile when it comes to ingredients—most of us have the basics of fresh onions, potatoes, and water.

Pair a soup with salad and crusty bread for a most satisfying and simple lunch or dinner. Perfect as a fast meal at work, soups travel well hot in a Thermos or cold in a microwavable container that can be reheated later.

Sausage and greens make this soup a wholesome, flavorful meal. Look for sausage with some spice—I used a turkey chorizo rather than sausage made from pork. The greens can be Swiss chard, kale, or even spinach. Roll the leaves like a cigar and cut into ⅛-inch-thick pieces to make chiffonade. *If you like your potatoes firm, use white or red boiling potatoes. If russets are all you've got, cut the pieces a little bigger and watch them closely while cooking so they don't get too mushy. For a hearty soup like this, I like the added flavor of potato skin.*

1 tablespoons olive oil

4 cups finely diced onions, about 2 medium-large onions

2 large cloves garlic, finely minced

6 large boiling potatoes, cut into ½-inch cubes, about 5 to 6 cups

8 cups water *or* chicken stock, *or* a mix

6 to 8 cups chiffonade of greens such as Swiss chard, escarole, kale, *or* a mix

½ pound spicy sausage such as chorizo *or* linguisa, cooked and cut in ½-inch-thick rounds

Salt and pepper, to taste

In a large pot, heat olive oil, add onions, and cook on

medium heat until soft, about 10 minutes. Add garlic and cook another 2 minutes.

Add potatoes and water or chicken stock, heat to boiling, then reduce heat. Simmer until potatoes are almost tender about 10 to 15 minutes depending on size of potato pieces.

Add greens and sausage and simmer a few minutes more. Taste and season with salt and pepper. Serve immediately.

LEMON AND DILL POTATO SALAD

Perk up a picnic or party with potatoes, cooked and served cold as a salad. This is a delicious and uncomplicated version that uses dill and lemon as the seasoning. I've used a little nonfat sour cream to bind the salad. For a richer salad, use nonfat or lowfat mayonnaise.

To cut time and cleanup, use leftover boiled or baked russets or new potatoes, or a mix, or microwave the potatoes, rather than boiling them on the stove. They take just minutes to microwave—be sure to check your manufacturer's instructions—then all you need to do is cut the potatoes into chunks. I prefer to leave the skins on for the additional flavor and texture.

3 pounds potatoes, cooked, cooled, and cut into small chunks

4 large green onions *or* ½ small red onion, finely chopped

¼ cup, *or* to taste, nonfat sour cream *or* mayonnaise

1 teaspoon dried dill weed *or* seed *or* about 1 tablespoon fresh snipped dill weed

Zest and juice of 1 large lemon

Salt and pepper, to taste

1 tablespoon chopped fresh parsley, for garnish

Put the potatoes in a large bowl. Mix remaining ingredients, except parsley, in a small bowl. Taste for proper seasoning, and then gently mix into the potatoes.

Cover and refrigerate at least a few hours to let the flavors meld. Serve with parsley sprinkled on top.

HERBED POTATOES

SERVES 4

Bored with the same old boiled and baked potato? This dish is a cinch to prepare and satisfying to boot. The potatoes are pre-cooked—on the stove or in the microwave oven—then quickly tossed with herbs and a bit of oil in a heavy skillet. The dish is a terrific addition to grilled meats, fish, or poultry.

Use red potatoes if possible; russets tend to crumble more during cooking. This recipe can be the base for any number of flavorful variations. Keep the main ingredients of potatoes and garlic, then vary the herbs to suit your taste and complement the particular meal you're serving. For an Italian twist, try rosemary, sage, thyme, or oregano. Whole spices and herbs such as mustard, cumin, and fennel seeds give an Indian touch to the potatoes.

1 tablespoon vegetable oil

4 cloves garlic, sliced

Small piece fresh ginger, finely chopped, optional

½ teaspoon mustard seeds

¼ teaspoon cumin seeds

1½ pounds red potatoes, quartered, steamed, boiled, *or* microwaved to fork doneness

Salt and pepper, to taste

2 sprigs fresh parsley *or* cilantro, finely chopped

In a large skillet, heat oil and add garlic and ginger. Cook on medium heat until garlic begins to soften and turn golden.

Add seeds and continue cooking another minute, or until seeds begin to pop. Add potatoes, salt, and pepper, toss, and cook about 3 minutes to heat through. Toss with parsley, taste for correct seasonings, and serve.

SAVORY POTATO WAFFLES

MAKES 5 OR 6 (6 × 10-INCH) WAFFLES; SERVES 8, ½ WAFFLE EACH

These savory potato waffles are a light and delicious twist on latkes (potato pancakes).

Two things make the waffles appealing. First, to save time, they can be frozen and reheated. Second, they need very little oil and are still crunchy. These waffles were inspired by a recipe in Sunset.

Serve the waffles with lowfat sour cream and applesauce or with sugar and cinnamon. Try them cut in bite-size pieces as finger food with drinks or as a snack. They also make an unusual side dish with poultry or meat.

I like my potatoes unpeeled. Use the food processor to chop the onion and parsley, then to shred the potatoes. Apples are also available at good prices and are great for homemade applesauce.

1 large onion, chopped
6 sprigs fresh parsley, chopped
8 medium russet potatoes, approximately 3 pounds, scrubbed and shredded
Juice of 1 lemon
4 eggs, separated, whites beaten stiff and yolks gently mixed
2 tablespoons fruity olive oil
⅔ cup unbleached, all-purpose flour
4 teaspoons baking powder
½ teaspoon cinnamon, optional
Salt and pepper, to taste

Working quickly so potatoes don't turn brown from the air, put onion, parsley, and potatoes into a large strainer or colander. With your hands, squeeze the liquid from the mixture. Put mixture into a bowl and add lemon juice. Mix with a fork.

Add egg yolks, oil, flour, baking powder, cinnamon (if using), salt, and pepper. Mix to blend. Quickly fold in egg whites.

Heat waffle iron according to manufacturer's instructions.

Spread mixture (about ½–¾ cup) evenly on iron and cook for about 10 minutes or until dark golden.

If making ahead, cool completely and freeze. Reheat in toaster or 300 degree F oven until crisp, about 10 minutes.

PUMPKIN WITH RICE AND GINGER

MAKES 4 GENEROUS CUPS

This holiday season, dare to be different . . . with pumpkin, that is. Rather than serve it as dessert, try the purée in this savory side dish. Cooked with rice and jazzed up with the flavors of fresh ginger, orange, and nutmeg, it's a low-cost, high-fiber, lowfat dish that's perfect with roast turkey and all the trimmings. For this easy-to-prepare, fast-cooking, and colorful dish, use puréed pumpkin (it's less than a buck a can and contains no additives).

There are numerous ways to add flavor and texture to this dish. Try the sweet taste of raisins and the subtle crunch of walnuts. Vary the liquid: Orange (or apple) juice lends a faintly fruity flavor while chicken broth adds richness. Water is always a neutral option. I like the flavors unadorned save for a final sprinkling of chopped parsley. The make-ahead dish can be cooked in a microwave oven; just follow manufacturer's instructions.

1 teaspoon olive oil
½ medium onion, finely
   chopped
1 scant tablespoon grated
   fresh ginger
1 cup raw rice
2½ cups liquid (I use 1 cup
   orange juice and 1½ cups
   water)
1 cup pumpkin purée
Salt and pepper, to taste
¼ teaspoon nutmeg, *or* to
   taste
1 heaping tablespoon
   chopped fresh parsley

¼ cup raisins, optional
2 tablespoons walnuts *or*
   pecans, chopped, optional

In a large saucepan, heat olive oil and add onion and ginger. Cook on medium heat for a few minutes until the onion begins to soften.

Add rice and stir well for about 1 minute. Then add liquid, pumpkin, salt, pepper, and nutmeg. Stir again to evenly mix. Bring to a boil, cover, and cook on medium-low heat for about 20 minutes *or* until liquid is absorbed. Stir and taste for correct seasoning. Serve sprinkled with parsley and raisins and nuts, if desired.

TO CHEW ON

Of soup and love, the first is best.
—Spanish Proverb

PUMPKIN PIE

SERVES 6 TO 8

True confession: I'm not a big pie fan. Making crusts from scratch is not my idea of fun, and pumpkin pie, in particular was never high on my list of favorites. Then I tasted this pie and realized how easy it is to make. A recipe by Craig Claiborne inspired me.

If you love making pie crusts, go ahead, or buy an unbaked 9-inch pie shell (look for one without preservatives or lard). When I first made this pie, I had no molasses on hand, so I left it out. I found this disappears just as quickly with or without it.

I have always made the pie with nonfat milk with very good results and a lot less fat and guilt. You can always add a scoop of ice cream or whipped cream. Higher fat milk results in a much richer and more caloric pie.

2 large eggs
½ cup sugar
2 tablespoons molasses, optional
½ teaspoon salt
1 tablespoon pumpkin pie spice blend
2 cups canned pumpkin
1½ cups nonfat milk, milk, or light cream
Unbaked 9-inch pie crust

Preheat oven to 450 degrees F.

Beat eggs with sugar, molasses (if using), salt, and spices until well blended. Add pumpkin and milk and mix well. Adjust seasonings.

Turn mixture into unbaked crust and bake on the lower shelf of oven for 10 minutes. Reduce temperature to 400 degrees F and bake about 30 minutes longer, until a knife inserted in the center comes out clean. Cool and serve plain, with whipped cream, or vanilla ice cream.

PUMPKIN SPICE CAKE

MAKES 24 LARGE PIECES

This easy cake is a lighter alternative to the usual rich pumpkin pie. It doesn't require a mixer, and it's great for the kids to make. It's dense because of the pumpkin and works well alone or with a dollop of whipped cream. I also like to serve it with stewed fruit such as pears or apples.

¾ cup butter (1½ sticks)
2 cups unbleached, all-purpose flour
1 cup sugar
1 teaspoon baking soda
2 teaspoons pumpkin pie spice *or* 1 heaping teaspoon cinnamon and ½ teaspoon *each* cloves and nutmeg
Zest of 1 orange, optional
1 cup canned pumpkin
1 egg, lightly beaten
1½ cups buttermilk
1 cup raisins, optional
½ cup chopped walnuts
½ cup chocolate chips, coarsely chopped

Preheat oven to 375 degrees F.

Grease a 12 × 10-inch jelly-roll pan.

Combine butter, flour, and sugar in bowl, and with hands, rub to crumbs. Add baking soda, spices, and zest (if using). Gently mix.

In another bowl, mix pumpkin, egg, and buttermilk together. Add to dry ingredients with raisins (if using) and walnuts. Gently stir with fork to incorporate liquid. Do not overmix. Dough will be thick.

Pour into prepared pan and gently spread. Sprinkle chocolate chips on top.

Bake for 25 minutes or until cake springs back when lightly touched.

RED AND WHITE RADISH SALAD

This snappy side dish makes a colorful and delicious accompaniment to grilled or roasted fish, meat, or poultry. The salad is simplicity itself: Fresh vegetables are shredded or finely chopped and dressed with a fruity olive oil and a dash of salt. It takes minutes to prepare, and, of course, can be done with your favorite vegetables.

The long skinny white daikon radish is widely available in the supermarket and tends not to be as hot as the small round red radishes. For color and crunch, add a shredded carrot or a peeled, seeded, and chopped cucumber. Don't add salt and pepper until serving time or the vegetables will get soggy. Serve individually in a red cabbage leaf, if desired.

1 medium white daikon radish, about ¾ pound, peeled and shredded,
1 small bunch red radishes, cleaned and shredded
1 small carrot, shredded, optional
1 small cucumber, peeled, seeded, and chopped, optional

2 to 3 teaspoons fruity olive oil, *or* to taste
Dash salt, *or* to taste
Black pepper, to taste

Toss vegetables in a bowl with olive oil. Just before serving, add salt and pepper.

SERVES 6

Try this toothsome dish with scrambled eggs and tortillas, roast meat, fish, or poultry. A little fruity olive oil, with the tomato juice, adds flavor to this lowfat dish. The dish was inspired by one by James Beard.

When seasoning this dish, be aware of the sodium in the tomato juice and adjust the amount of added salt as necessary for your taste. For extra spiciness, add your favorite salsa. The sugar helps cut the high acidity of the tomato juice. If Mexican herbs don't please your palate, try Italian herb blend and skip the optional salsa. Serve with cheese and lime wedges on the side for an extra flavor zip.

1 onion, finely sliced
2 cloves garlic, pressed
2 teaspoons fruity olive oil
1½ teaspoons Mexican herb blend, *or* chile powder
1 teaspoon sugar, *or* to taste
1 (4 ounce) can sliced olives
1 cup uncooked long-grain rice
Salt and pepper, to taste
2 tablespoons salsa, optional
4 cups tomato juice, heated to boiling
3 sprigs parsley *or* cilantro, finely chopped
Parmesan *or* shredded Cheddar cheese, optional for the table
Lime wedges, optional for the table

Preheat oven to 350 degrees F.

In a 2-quart baking dish, place all ingredients except parsley, cheese, and lime. Stir to combine.

Bake, uncovered, for about 20 minutes. Gently stir and taste to check doneness of rice and correctness of flavor. Continue cooking a few minutes more, if necessary.

Remove from oven and serve sprinkled with chopped parsley or cilantro.

BRUNCH RICE

What food does two-thirds of the world's population consume as their main staple? Rice. Much of the world eats rice as a main dish with vegetables and very little, if any, meat. Raw rice is versatile; cheap; fat-, sodium-, and cholesterol-free; and easy to digest.

Look for raw rice in the see-through packages at about $1.30 for 2 pounds, or 32 half-cup servings. Try to avoid packages of processed convenience rice with additives that sell for about $1.25 and contain only 5 half-cup servings.

Whether raw or convenience, most rice cooks in 15 to 20 minutes. For fluffy separate grains, use long-grain varieties; for creamier or slightly stickier rice, use medium or short grain.

This recipe makes a hearty side dish for brunch or a main course for a light dinner. Serve with a salad, bread, and dessert for a simple and toothsome meal.

Plain Rice
Cook rice according to package instructions or this easy way:

1 cup uncooked rice
1¾ to 2 cups water *or* broth
1 teaspoon salt, optional
1 tablespoon butter *or* oil, optional

Put all ingredients in a 2- to 3-quart saucepan. Bring to a boil, stir once, reduce heat, cover, and simmer for 15 minutes. This yields 3 to 4 cups cooked rice. Cooked rice keeps 6 to 7 days refrigerated in a tightly covered container.

1 sweet Italian sausage, *or* your favorite, about ¼ to ⅓ pound bulk, casing removed, broken into small pieces
1 large carrot, shredded
8 medium mushrooms, *or* ¼ pound, sliced
4 medium green onions, finely chopped, *or* ½ medium onion, finely chopped
4 eggs

¼ cup skim *or* lowfat milk
Salt and pepper, to taste
½ teaspoon Italian seasoning
   blend, *or* to taste, optional
3 cups cooked rice
4 tablespoons grated Parmesan cheese
2 tablespoons chopped fresh
   herb such as parsley or
   basil, optional for garnish

In a large nonstick skillet, cook sausage until browned. Drain and return meat to skillet.

Add carrot, mushrooms, and onions and cook on medium heat, stirring occasionally, about 2 minutes or until vegetables begin to wilt.

In a bowl, mix eggs, milk, salt, pepper, and spices. Pour eggs over vegetables. Stir and cook on medium heat about 1½ minutes or until eggs just begin to set.

Turn heat to medium low, add rice and cheese, and stir to heat though.

Serve immediately sprinkled with fresh herbs.

TO-YOUR-TASTE RICE SALAD

SERVES 4; DRESSING MAKES ABOUT ½ CUP

Try this colorful salad for lunch or dinner. Let it stand alone as a side dish or serve it as a main course with a salad. Low-cost and versatile, rice mixes with virtually any vegetable so use your taste and imagination to create your own version of this salad. In the recipe given here, prepared for the Mexican festival of Cinco de Mayo, I give the dish a south-of-the-border flavor by using cumin, a pinch of oregano, and coriander.

Herbs and spices are one key to changing the salad to suit your needs. Curry, ginger and garlic make it Indian, while cumin, oregano, cilantro, and garlic give a Mexican flavor. Fresh basil, parsley, garlic, and oregano move it into the Italian arena; and ginger, garlic, sesame oil, and soy sauce create Asian flavors.

Try different seasonal vegetables for more variations. Don't forget that frozen corn kernels or peas are available year-round at reasonable prices. Use raw rice (about $1.30 for a 2-pound package) cooked according to package instructions. It will take about 20 minutes.

Consider a seasonal presentation—in April, May, and June, use a cold artichoke; later during the summer, try green or red bell peppers or hollowed-out tomatoes.

3 cups plain cooked rice, cold
1 small carrot, shredded
3 medium green onions, finely chopped
½ cup green peas, cooked
½ cup corn kernels, cooked
½ red, green, or yellow bell pepper, optional

2 tablespoons chopped almonds and/or walnuts, lightly toasted, optional
1 (15-ounce) can black beans, rinsed, optional

Mix all ingredients and dress with favorite dressing, or this one:

Dressing

For a slightly sweeter variation, use orange juice. Use fresh herbs when possible and to your taste.

Juice and zest of 1 large lemon, about 4 tablespoons
2 tablespoons vegetable oil
1 large clove garlic, pressed
Dash Worcestershire sauce
2 tablespoons finely chopped fresh parsley *or* cilantro
1 teaspoon ground cumin *or* your favorite Mexican blend

¼ teaspoon *each* oregano and coriander, *or* use Mexican blend
Salt and pepper, to taste
Dash cayenne, to taste

Mix all ingredients, taste for correct seasoning, and pour over rice. Mix well. Chill, taste again, and adjust the flavoring as the rice soaks up the flavors. Serve on red cabbage leaves, stuffed in an artichoke, or in a large bowl.

SERVES 6 TO 8

Juk rhymes with "hook." David owns SooHoo's, a fast and healthy Chinese restaurant in Sacramento, California. This dish has its ethnic roots in China where it is called congee or juk. It's eaten for breakfast or when one is feeling under the weather. I think it's great anytime.

Make this thick and creamy soup as a satisfying winter main course or as a side dish with vegetables or meat. It's comfort food—as easy to make as it is to eat. Begin it in a Crock-Pot on low heat in the morning and it will be ready to serve for dinner.

Add bite-size pieces of mushrooms, broccoli, or small pieces of chicken marinated in egg white and soy sauce to cook during the last fifteen minutes. Long-grain rice works, but the texture is silkier with medium-grain.

Elaine's favorite way to eat this dish is to first add a dash of oyster sauce and a sprinkling of chopped green onion and cilantro.

Note: *Soy milk is an optional addition that makes the dish white and creamy. Be sure to use plain soy milk, not the drink or beverage. If it's unavailable in the supermarket, try health food or Asian food markets.*

1 cup medium- or long-grain rice
Water to soak rice
1 tablespoon vegetable oil (not olive)
6 cups chicken stock *or* turkey stock
6 cups water
1 teaspoon salt
1 chicken breast cut in bite size pieces, marinated in an egg white and a few teaspoons of soy sauce
2 cups soy milk, optional, see note above

4 green onions, finely chopped, for garnish

½ bunch fresh cilantro, finely chopped, for garnish

Soak rice in water to cover for 30 minutes. Rinse and drain.

In a large pot, heat oil, add rice, and sauté for a few minutes.

Add stock, water, and salt. Bring to a boil, then simmer for 1½ to 2 hours uncovered, stirring occasionally. Be sure the heat is very low, or you will burn the rice.

Add chicken during the last 15 minutes of cooking. Rice mixture should be thick and pasty.

If using soy milk, add, stir, bring to a boil and cook for a few minutes.

Serve with small bowls of chopped green onions and cilantro and a bottle of oyster sauce on the table.

RICE WITH BUTTERNUT SQUASH

SERVES 2 TO 3 AS A MAIN COURSE

This toothsome recipe uses two of my favorite foods: winter squash—in this case butternut—and rice. The rice used is a medium-grain white Italian rice with a certain amount of starch that allows the grains to cling but not get gummy. Arborio is the most common variety—it is a bit more expensive than regular long-grain rice. Look for it in the ethnic foods section of the supermarket or at an Italian grocery.

This is a satisfying dish when paired with a green salad and perhaps a poached pear for dessert (page 184). If you choose to use chicken broth, use it the same way as the water. You'll need about 4 to 5 cups of liquid.

Note: *My mom hates stirring constantly. For an equally delicious dish, she uses long-grain rice, covers the pot, cooks it on low heat, and stirs only occasionally. If necessary, she adds liquid.*

2 or 3 tablespoons butter *or* olive oil
1 teaspoon salt, plus more to taste
1 onion, finely chopped
1 large clove garlic, minced
1 teaspoon Italian herb blend
1 cup long-grain *or* arborio medium-grain Italian rice
1 small butternut squash, peeled, seeded, and diced (about 1 pound prepared weight)
½ cup dry white wine, optional

Pinch ground nutmeg, *or* to taste
2 or 3 tablespoons grated Parmesan cheese
Black pepper, to taste

Fill a kettle with water, bring it to a boil, then keep it simmering. Melt butter or olive oil in a large nonstick wok or skillet on a medium flame. Stir in the salt, onion, garlic, and herbs. When the onion turns translucent, add rice. Stir the rice until the rice turns clear.

Stir in the squash, then wine (if using) or a splash of boiling water from the kettle. Stir until liquid evaporates, then pour in more water ½ cup at a time. Continue adding liquid and stirring occasionally.

After 20 minutes, check rice and squash for doneness. When rice is chewy and squash tender, remove pan from heat. Add nutmeg and Parmesan a little at a time, stirring vigorously to develop the creaminess of the rice. Taste and adjust seasonings, season with ground pepper, and serve immediately.

SERVES 6

Usher in the New Year with a French twist for a simple and hearty dish. Two unlikely ingredients—Champagne and sauerkraut—partner with smoked meat and boiled potatoes. When served, the ingredients are placed around a small bottle of Champagne on the serving platter. The heat from the platter and the foods warms the liquid, which bubbles out of the open bottle onto the sauerkraut. This delightfully aromatic dish is a favorite of Sacramento grocer, Darrell Corti.

Look for bulk sauerkraut at delicatessens or in the deli section of the supermarket. Canned sauerkraut works, but not as well. Note, the sauerkraut is rinsed to remove some of the brine. Serve on a platter with sausages, smoked chicken, turkey, or pork loin and boiled or steamed potatoes. Although there seems to be a lot of alcohol in the dish, it cooks out, leaving the essence of its flavor with the sauerkraut. A California sparkling wine easily works instead of the Champagne.

2 tablespoons butter

1 large onion, peeled and thinly sliced

2 medium carrots, scraped and thinly sliced

2 pounds fresh bulk sauerkraut, rinsed and squeezed dry

1 bay leaf

8 juniper berries *or* 2 shots gin

1 cup white wine *or* beer

2 cups stock (beef, chicken, *or* vegetable, low sodium, if possible

1 piece smoked meat such as ham hock, bacon rind, bacon ends, *or* smoked turkey leg

Salt and freshly ground pepper, to taste

1 glass sparkling wine

Preheat oven to 350 degrees F.

In a large ovenproof pot with a cover, melt the butter and add the onion and carrots. Cover and cook on medium heat until soft, about 5 minutes.

Add sauerkraut, bay leaf, and berries or gin. Raise the heat to medium-high and add wine or beer, stock, and meat. Cook for a few minutes to incorporate flavors. Stir, cover, and bake 1½ to 2 hours. Not much liquid should be left. If there is, uncover and cook about a half hour. Taste for correct seasoning. Add salt and pepper to taste.

Serve on a large platter surround by meats and potatoes, and pour the glass of sparkling wine over the sauerkraut. Or serve it as noted above with a small bottle of sparkling wine, opened and bubbling over from the heat of food.

MAKES 40 TO 48 PIECES TO SERVE 6 TO 8

Perfect with beer and drinks, sausage makes great finger food. Serve versatile sausages as a main course or use a little to flavor soups, salads, vegetables, and casseroles. Many sausages are previously cooked by smoking and need only to be heated through by frying, grilling, or simmering. Fresh sausages take a little longer to cook. A pound of sausage is about $2.50 and each sausage cut-up makes 6 to 8 rounds or bites. Well-known sausage maker Bruce Aidells inspired these rounds.

¾ cup roasted peanuts *or* almonds, finely chopped

¾ cup finely chopped fresh parsley *or* cilantro

6 spicy sausages, such as turkey, bratwurst, kielbasa, bockwurst, *or* your favorite sausage

¾ cup mustard *or* sweet mango chutney

Mix nuts with parsley.

Fry sausages in a skillet over medium heat. Turn frequently and cook for about 10 minutes. Remove from pan, cut each into 6 to 8 bite-size pieces.

Serve immediately with toothpicks for each piece. Present sausage pieces on a platter, surrounded by bowls of mustard or chutney, and nut mixture. Guests dip the rounds first in mustard or chutney, then in the nut mixture.

To stretch the shrimp, shell and cut them horizontally to make two pieces, or cut them into smaller pieces. For a main course, serve this dish over rice.

Shrimp make great finger food, whether shelled or unshelled. Look for sambal oelek (chile paste) in the Asian foods section of the supermarket, or at an Asian foods specialty store. To stay on budget, look for shrimp on special at the supermarket. If light soy sauce seems too salty, try diluting it with a tablespoon of water to use in the recipe. Try recipe with scallops or chunks of fish such as snapper.

1 tablespoon vegetable oil
2 large cloves garlic, finely chopped
1 small piece ginger, finely chopped, if desired
½ pound raw shrimp with shells, deveined, if necessary
1 tablespoon light soy sauce
1 teaspoon Asian-style chile paste such as sambal oelek, *or* dried red pepper flakes
Juice of ¼ large lemon, *or* to taste
1 tablespoon sugar, *or* to taste

In a skillet or wok, heat oil on medium-high heat. Add garlic and ginger. Stir-fry until golden. Turn heat to high, add shrimp so each lies flat and the shell begins to crisp. Toss so shrimp cook quickly, and as they turn pink, add soy sauce, chile paste, lemon juice, and sugar. Toss until sauce glazes shrimp.

Serve hot or at room temperature.

SPINACH AND PASTA SALAD

MAKES ABOUT 4 CUPS, SERVES 8
DRESSING MAKES ⅔ CUP

When summer's heat makes it almost too hot to eat, salads make easy light meals that take little preparation. This simple pasta salad combines spinach and cabbage to create a tasty and colorful mix. It can be served as a side dish or as a main course.

The dressing can be your favorite or this unusual one with orange and ginger. Rather than using spinach leaves whole, roll the leaves together and cut them into thin ribbons. Leftover meat or poultry can be added to make a main dish, if desired.

1 bunch fresh spinach, washed, dried, and stemmed

½ pound pasta, spirals *or* shells, cooked and cooled

¼ head red cabbage, finely shredded

½ red onion, finely chopped

2 tablespoons finely chopped fresh parsley

1 cup leftover meat, cut *or* shredded into bite-size pieces, optional

Take a small handful of spinach leaves and roll them lengthwise to make a bundle. Finely cut into ½-inch pieces to make ribbons.

Put all ingredients in a large bowl and toss with orange-ginger dressing. Serve chilled or at room temperature.

Orange-Ginger Dressing

⅔ cup orange juice, about 2 oranges

Zest of 1 orange

1 small piece fresh ginger, chopped, about 1 heaping teaspoon

1 teaspoon sugar, *or* to taste

Pinch ground cloves *or* cinnamon, *or* to taste

2 tablespoons cider *or* white vinegar, *or* to taste

2 teaspoons fruity olive oil, optional

Salt and pepper, to taste

Put all ingredients in a small saucepan and bring to a boil. Cool slightly, taste for correct seasoning, and pour over salad.

CREAMY SPINACH PESTO

This is a variation of Sarah's Zucchini Sauce (page 258) using spinach in place of zucchini.

Pesto to many means the traditional deliciously addictive mixture of fresh basil, olive oil, garlic, and Parmesan cheese. These days, a slew of innovative new combos are springing up in restaurants and cookbooks.

4 cups well-packed spinach *or* fresh basil *or* part basil and parsley leaves, washed and spun dry, approximately 1 large bunch of spinach

2 green onions, chopped

2 cloves garlic

2 tablespoons chopped fresh parsley

¾ cup water *or* vegetable broth

1 cup lowfat ricotta cheese

3 tablespoons freshly grated Parmesan cheese

Salt and pepper, to taste

Put spinach leaves, green onions, garlic, parsley, and broth or water in a food processor. Process until coarsely chopped, about 30 seconds, scraping down sides if necessary. Add cheeses, salt, and pepper. Process until creamy, about 20 seconds.

Serve immediately. Good over pasta.

SPINACH AND SPAGHETTI SQUASH SAUTÉ

SERVES 4 TO 6

Question: What do pasta and winter squash have in common?

Answer: They both include a variety called spaghetti.

Spaghetti made from flour is one thing, but a squash masquerading as spaghetti is quite another. When cooked, the yellow-skinned, football-shaped winter squash yields golden strands resembling pasta.

This simple recipe pairs squash and spinach with the exotic flavors of Indian curry, garlic, and ginger. Note that curry powders vary in flavor and intensity. Definitely sample the cooked dish and adjust the seasoning according to your taste. For an Italian-flavored variation, substitute basil, garlic, and a little Parmesan cheese for the curry and ginger.

This easy sauté can be made in a nonstick skillet. To cook the squash, use the microwave oven or boil or steam it on the stovetop, until just soft. Cut the cooked squash in half, remove the seeds, and lift the strands out, leaving the hard outer shell.

Serve the dish with rice and a big salad for a vegetarian meal, or use the sauté as a side dish with fish, meat, or poultry. The dish tastes terrific without the optional ingredients, though in any combination they add an additional flavor and textural dimension.

2 teaspoons vegetable oil, optional if using nonstick skillet

1 small piece fresh ginger, finely chopped

2 cloves garlic, finely chopped

1 medium onion, finely sliced

½ to 1 teaspoon curry powder, *or* to taste

1 bunch fresh spinach, stemmed, rinsed, left with water clinging, coarsely chopped

1 medium spaghetti squash, boiled *or* steamed, seeded, and peeled
Salt and pepper, to taste
1 heaping tablespoon raisins, optional
1 heaping tablespoon chopped toasted almonds, optional
4 sprigs fresh cilantro, finely chopped, optional
Few leaves fresh mint, finely chopped *or* ½ teaspoon dried, optional

In a large skillet, heat oil and add ginger, garlic, onion, and curry powder. Cook on medium heat until onions begin to soften, about 2 to 3 minutes.

Add spinach, toss to combine with onion mixture. Cover and let cook until spinach begins to wilt.

Add squash, salt, pepper, and optional ingredients, if using. Mix and continue to cook until spinach is just wilted. Add any optional ingredients.

Toss, and taste for correct seasoning. Serve with rice.

MAKES ABOUT 16

East meets West with these seasonal and versatile winter squash raviolis. Wonton wrappers encase the winter squash or pumpkin purée, and the bundles are served with a drizzle of browned butter and a sprinkle of Parmesan. The flavors are meant to be simple and not overwhelming. For another variation, fry them in oil to serve with a zippy chutney dip as finger food with drinks.

Look for in-season butternut, acorn, or banana squash or canned pumpkin in the supermarket—all of these are a good buy during the winter holidays. Serve the dish for a dressy accompaniment to the Thanksgiving or Hanukkah meal.

To cook squash, bake, microwave, or steam it until soft. Peel off the outer shell and mash the flesh. Make the bundles ahead and freeze them. Look for fresh wonton wrappers in the produce section of the supermarket or at Asian food markets.

1 cup canned pumpkin *or* cooked and mashed butternut, banana, or acorn squash
1 clove garlic, pressed
¼ to ½ teaspoon ground nutmeg, *or* to taste
1 tablespoon finely minced fresh parsley
Salt and pepper, to taste
32 wonton wrappers
Small bowl of water
4 tablespoons butter
1 heaping teaspoon dried sage *or* a few fresh leaves
2 tablespoons Parmesan cheese

In a bowl, mix all ingredients except wrappers, water, butter, sage, and cheese. Taste for correct seasoning.

Lay out 16 wrappers on a dry work space. Put a heaping teaspoon of filling on each wrapper. Working quickly, dip a finger in water and run it around the edge of the wrapper. Cover filling with another wrapper and seal the wet edges.

Continue to make bundles. Do not stack them.

At this point, bundles can be frozen. Line a baking sheet with waxed paper or aluminum foil. Put bundles on in a single layer and freeze for a few hours. Then store them in a plastic freezer bag. Do not defrost before cooking.

To fry: Use a nonstick skillet with a tablespoon or so of oil. On medium heat, fry the wontons slowly to heat through but not burn. Turn and brown on other side. Cooking should take about 5 to 7 minutes. Drain on paper towels and serve with a bowl of chutney for dip.

To boil: Bring a large pot of water to boil. Put six or eight bundles in the water and cook until they rise to the top, about 1 or 2 minutes. If frozen, cook a few minutes more. Remove from water with slotted spoon and drain in a colander.

To serve, cook butter with sage in a small saucepan on medium heat until butter is slightly browned, not burned. Drizzle mixture over bundles and sprinkle with Parmesan cheese.

TOMATO-VEGETABLE SOUP

MAKES ABOUT 12 CUPS; ABOUT 1 CUP PER PERSON

Winter months bring fresh tomatoes high in price and anemically low in flavor and color, so I don't buy them. Instead, I turn to my cupboard for canned tomato products. Tomato or vegetable juice (low sodium or regular) is the backbone of this delicious meal-in-one soup. Add any favorite seasonal or fresh-frozen vegetables, some cooked beans, or a handful of uncooked rice or small pasta for texture and flavor.

For a smaller quantity, use a smaller can of juice, and cut the ingredients accordingly. This fat-free soup (without the cheese) also freezes well. Serve with crusty bread and a salad.

1 (48-ounce) can tomato *or* vegetable juice
2½ cups water
1 (14-ounce) can chopped tomatoes
2 medium onions, finely chopped
3 stalks celery, thinly sliced crosswise
3 carrots, thinly sliced
1 small head cabbage, shredded
¼ cup chopped fresh parsley
4 cloves garlic, pressed
2 bay leaves
1 heaping teaspoon dried Italian herb blend, *or* to taste
Dash red pepper flakes, optional
Salt and black pepper, to taste

1 cup raw pasta *or* rice, optional
Grated Parmesan cheese to serve on the side, optional

In a large stockpot, put all ingredients except pasta or rice and cheese. Bring to a boil, then cover and simmer for about 20 to 30 minutes or until vegetables soften.

If using pasta, check cooking instructions on package and add it accordingly before cooking is finished. Added rice takes about 20 minutes to cook so it could be added about 10 minutes into the cooking.

Taste for correct seasoning. Serve with cheese in a bowl on the side, if desired.

SERVES 4 TO 6

How can a dish so simple taste so good? Because it's made in the summer when tomatoes are ripe red (or yellow) and juicy. Figure one medium tomato per person. Mix varieties and colors when available. If you don't have fresh herbs, try a bit of dried. If the tomatoes are spectacular, let them stand alone without the herbs.

*Serve as a salad or a topping for lightly grilled or toasted bread (*bruschetta*) or as a salsa for grilled meat, fish, or poultry.*

4 tomatoes, halved and cut in small pieces, including juice

Handful of fresh parsley, basil, *or* thyme, finely chopped

Salt and pepper, to taste

1 or 2 tablespoons olive oil, *or* to taste

1 or 2 tablespoons balsamic *or* favorite vinegar

Mix all ingredients. Taste for correct seasoning and let rest, if possible, ½ hour to meld the flavors.

MAKES 4

Give fast food a new spin with these tortilla-wrapped vegetable bundles. Put colorful vegetables and fruits in a tortilla for a quick, colorful, and easy light meal, snack, appetizer, or party food.

These wraps won't create havoc with your food budget, especially if you use on-hand foods and your imagination. The possible fillings are innumerable, and with a judicious use of cheese or meat, fat can be kept to a minimum. Kids love a slather of peanut butter, banana or apple, raisins, and a sprinkling of cinnamon, while adults gobble up any of the combos with drinks.

Think color and crunch—the basic four vegetables for these wraps are cabbage, carrot, onion, and sprouts. Some possible combos include peanut butter, curry blend, and basic four; light cream cheese, Italian herb blend, and basic four; peanut butter, cinnamon, apple or banana, and raisins. Try adding other vegetables for color and texture, including radishes (red and white daikon), potatoes, red onion, olives, artichoke hearts. I make my own bean dip with a can of drained and rinsed pinto, garbanzo, or kidney beans (see Fast Bean Dip, page 55). Mash or purée them with garlic and spices and a little salsa to taste.

To make the rolls pretty when cut, lay a single line of each ingredient rather than mushing them all together.

1 package lowfat flour tortillas, burrito size	6 medium green onions, shredded in 1-inch lengths
½ cup (2 tablespoons per tortilla) bean dip *or* spread of choice	2 cups shredded red cabbage
	2 medium carrots, shredded
½ to 1 teaspoon Mexican blend herbs	2 cups alfalfa sprouts
	Salt and pepper, to taste

On each tortilla, spread about 2 tablespoons dip. Sprinkle with herbs. Divide green onion slivers into 4 portions. For each tortilla use ½ cup each of the vegetables and a portion of onion. Lay each side by side, and season, if desired with salt and pepper.

Roll tightly and adhere edge with a little dip, if necessary. Wrap in plastic wrap and refrigerate to set flavors.

To serve, cut on diagonal—in half—or in 1½-inch pieces, about 6 per tortilla.

TURKEY AND PITA BREAD SANDWICH

Turkey in August! Of course, because turkey isn't only for Thanksgiving—it's available year-round. This easy dish combines summer vegetables and ground turkey in pita bread. Serve it on a buffet so guests can make their own sandwich. The dish works well cooked on the barbecue—make patties rather than balls out of the turkey mixture.

If available, use fresh herbs to give an extra boost to the mixture; use approximately 1 tablespoon fresh for 1 teaspoon dried. The meatballs make an easy hors d'oeuvre when served on toothpicks and then dipped in the sauce. Make them ahead and warm them in a low oven before serving. Other additions to the sandwich could include sliced avocado, alfalfa sprouts, or shredded carrot.

Turkey Meatballs

1 package ground turkey meat, approximately 1 pound

¼ medium onion, finely chopped

1 clove garlic, pressed

3 sprigs fresh parsley, finely chopped

1 teaspoon dried mint

1 teaspoon dried oregano

Salt and pepper, to taste

1 to 3 teaspoons olive oil, optional for cooking

Mix all ingredients except oil together, then form into small balls. Use a nonstick skillet and cook the balls until brown. If desired, use 1 teaspoon olive oil to fry the balls. Or form into patties and broil or grill.

Sauce

½ cup nonfat yogurt, sour cream, *or* a blend of each

Few drops Tabasco sauce, *or* to taste

1 small clove garlic, pressed, *or* to taste

¼ cucumber, peeled, seeded, and finely chopped, optional

Mix all ingredients. Adjust seasoning to taste.

To Serve Sandwiches

3 (6-inch) pieces pita bread, sliced in half horizontally
1 medium tomato, finely chopped
6 lettuce leaves, chopped
2 medium green onions, finely chopped

Fill pita with tomato and lettuce, add a sprinkle of green onion, 2 or 3 meatballs, and top with a drizzle of sauce.

TURKEY FAJITAS

Thanksgiving means a terrific turkey dinner, and with a little planning, leftovers. If you've maxed out using leftover turkey in salads, soups, and sandwiches, try a different dish of fajitas.

The usual method for making fajitas is to marinate raw meat for grilling along with onions and peppers. In this easy recipe, the vegetables are marinated then stir-fried, and the leftover turkey is added in the final minutes of cooking.

Use corn or flour tortillas to wrap the mixture. Vary the ingredients according to what leftovers you have on hand and what vegetables you prefer. I like the kick of lime, but lemon also works. If fresh bell peppers are too expensive, use more onions and sliced carrots to add color and texture or try buying frozen sliced bell peppers. Added garnishes might include salsa, sour cream, or guacamole.

Juice of 1 lime, about 2 tablespoons

3 tablespoons orange juice *or* tequila

1 teaspoon dried oregano

1 teaspoon ground cumin

1 teaspoon chile powder

Dash cayenne

Salt and pepper, to taste

1 large onion, thinly sliced

1 green bell pepper, seeded and thinly sliced

2 medium carrots, thinly sliced

1 tablespoon *or* less vegetable oil

2 to 3 cups leftover cooked turkey, small chunks

4 sprigs cilantro, finely chopped

8 medium corn *or* flour tortillas, warmed

Make marinade of citrus juices, oregano, cumin, chile powder, cayenne, salt, and pepper.

Toss vegetables into mixture and let rest for an hour or so. Save the marinade.

Heat a nonstick or regular skillet with the oil. Add vegetables and stir-fry on high until they begin to soften, about 2 to 3 minutes. Be sure to constantly toss vegetables so they don't stick and burn. Add the turkey and marinade and continue cooking on medium-high until the turkey is warmed through. Add cilantro and toss.

Serve in warmed tortillas rolled with salsa and other condiments.

SERVES 4

For a versatile alternative to ground beef, try turkey. Its mild flavor makes it well-suited to most herbs and vegetables. You will generally find it priced at about $2 a pound—be sure to read the label for fat content. These patties are jazzed up with flavor, texture, and color from herbs and chopped vegetables.

A pound of meat easily serves four. Serve the patties on hamburger buns garnished with your favorite condiments. Or serve them as a hearty dinner with mashed potatoes and a salad. If you don't want to make patties, sauté the meat loose and add it to pasta, rice, or scrambled eggs as you would ground beef.

1 pound ground turkey
1 rib celery, finely chopped
¼ medium onion, finely chopped
3 sprigs fresh parsley *or* cilantro, finely chopped
1 large clove garlic, pressed
½ shredded carrot
1 heaping teaspoon herb blend, Italian, Mexican, curry, *or* your favorite

Salt and pepper, to taste
Dash Worcestershire sauce

Mix all ingredients well. Refrigerate, if possible, to let flavors meld.

Form into patties and sauté in a nonstick pan or a lightly greased skillet.

TURKEY AND POTATO PATTIES

Finish off leftover turkey and mashed potatoes with these patties. The measurements need not be exact and the vegetables and seasonings can vary.

2 cups mashed potatoes
2 cups cooked turkey, cut into bite-size pieces
½ medium onion, finely diced
½ small carrot, grated
1 small rib celery, finely diced
½ teaspoon Italian herb blend, to taste
1 egg white
1 tablespoon minced fresh parsley, *or* other herb, optional
Salt and pepper, to taste
⅓ cup unbleached, all-purpose flour for dipping the patties
2 to 3 tablespoons vegetable *or* olive oil

Mix all ingredients except the flour and oil.

Shape into patties. Put flour on a plate and dip patties once on each side to lightly coat with flour.

Place 1 to 2 tablespoons oil in a skillet, or use a nonstick pan with a teaspoon or two of oil, and heat on medium.

Cook patties until brown, turn, and brown other side, about 5 minutes. Use more oil, if necessary. Serve with a simple salad or vegetable.

SERVES 6

Winter vegetables make terrific side dishes. These include, among others, boiled or baked hard-skinned squashes (acorn, butternut, spaghetti), boiled or steamed root vegetables (carrots, parsnips, turnips, rutabagas, beets), and baked or boiled tubers (potatoes, yams, sweet potatoes). Winter vegetables are particularly appealing for taste, color, and price. Many of them run well under $1 a pound. And, russet potatoes are always available in five- and ten-pound bags at a low price.

If you choose the colorful yellow acorn or butternut squash for a side dish, simply cut the squash in half, sprinkle with a pinch of cinnamon and brown sugar, cover, and bake about 45 minutes to 1 hour in a 350 degree F oven, or until pulp is soft.

This recipe works with any combination of your favorite vegetables, though I prefer the sweetness of carrots along with the earthiness of potatoes, turnips, and rutabagas. Cook the vegetables to just soft, not mush. If you prefer, cook the vegetables separately and then combine them. The horseradish gives a zip so be sure to adjust the seasonings to your taste.

3 large carrots, peeled, cut into 1-inch pieces

4 to 5 medium potatoes, peeled, cut in eighths

1 or 2 turnips, peeled, cut in eighths

1 large rutabaga, peeled, cut in eighths

1 large onion, peeled, cut in eighths, layers peeled apart

2 to 4 tablespoons olive oil *or* butter, *or* to taste

1 small clove garlic, pressed

1 to 2 tablespoons prepared horseradish, *or* to taste

2 to 4 tablespoons cider vinegar, *or* to taste

1 heaping teaspoon dill, *or* to taste

Salt and pepper, to taste

1 tablespoon chopped fresh parsley, for garnish, optional

Fill a large pot with water and bring to a boil. Add the carrots and cook about 5 minutes.

Add the potatoes, turnips, and rutabaga, and continue cooking at a boil another 5 minutes or until the vegetables begin to soften. Finally, add the onion, cover, and turn heat to simmer.

Simmer another few minutes until the vegetables are cooked to your taste.

Remove pot from heat, drain vegetables, and put into a large bowl.

Heat remaining ingredients except parsley for about 30 seconds in a microwavable bowl or in a saucepan on the stove. Pour over the vegetables. Toss, season with salt and pepper, and adjust seasonings, if necessary. Serve warm or at room temperature, garnished, if desired, with a sprinkling of chopped parsley.

SERVES 4

Barbecue sauce is a summertime staple, usually spread on meats and poultry. In this easy recipe the sauce transforms summer mainstay vegetables—zucchini, peppers, eggplant, and tomatoes—into a simple, subtly flavored side dish or main course. Try the vegetables in a soft taco topped with chopped lettuce and a sprinkling of cheese. Spoon them over steamed rice for a meal or use alone as a side dish with grilled fish, meat, or chicken, or top on crusty French bread and serve as a light lunch.

Any favorite barbecue sauce will do—just don't overdo the amount you add to the vegetables. I found that a simple ready-made tomato-based sauce (without lots of ingredients) works very well. For extra zip, add a little fresh chopped jalapeño pepper. Vary the amounts of vegetables to your taste and their availability. Cook this lowfat, low-cost mix on the stovetop or in the microwave. Try not to serve the vegetables with barbecue-flavored meat or the meal will taste like barbecue sauce!

1 medium eggplant, cut in small cubes

1 medium onion, thinly sliced

½ green, red, *or* yellow bell pepper, thinly sliced

2 medium zucchini, thinly sliced

3 medium tomatoes, coarsely chopped

1 large clove garlic, pressed *or* finely chopped

1 to 2 tablespoons favorite tomato-based barbecue sauce, *or* to taste

Pinch of cayenne, dash of Tabasco sauce, *or* ½ seeded and finely chopped fresh jalapeño pepper, optional to taste

Salt and pepper, to taste

Few sprigs fresh parsley *or* cilantro, finely chopped for garnish

Put all ingredients, except parsley or cilantro, in a large saucepan. Cook on high heat until mixture begins to bubble, then turn to medium heat, stir, cover, and cook about 15 minutes or until vegetables are soft and mixture thickens slightly. Taste for correct seasoning. Serve warm sprinkled with parsley or cilantro.

LEMON–CUMIN VEGETABLE ROLLS

MAKES ABOUT 10, DEPENDING ON SIZE OF WRAPPERS

East meets West with these easy-to-prepare vegetable spring rolls. Fill the wrapper with a cabbage-based mixture that's spiced with cumin, lemon, and cilantro. Rather than deep-fry the rolls, try them sautéed in the barest amount of oil. The crunchy rolls, served with a spicy dip, make a delicious light Lenten lunch or dinner with soup and dessert.

Make the rolls ahead of time, freeze, and reheat, unthawed, in a 325 degree F oven. The dip is a cinch with your favorite bottled salsa mixed with plain nonfat yogurt or regular sour cream. Vary the vegetables according to taste, and try to think color and crunch. Leftover meat, or a few shrimp can easily embellish this simple dish. If bell peppers are not available fresh and at a reasonable price, look for them in the frozen food section.

3 teaspoons vegetable oil

1 small napa *or* round cabbage, finely shredded, about 7 cups

½ large onion, finely sliced

2 large cloves garlic, finely chopped

1 rib celery, finely diced

1 medium green, red, or yellow bell pepper, *or* a mixture, coarsely chopped, about 1 cup

1 scant teaspoon ground cumin

Salt and pepper, to taste

Dash Tabasco sauce, optional

1 small carrot, finely grated

Juice of half lemon, about 2 tablespoons

6 sprigs cilantro, finely chopped, about 2 tablespoons

Package of spring roll wrappers

1 cup nonfat sour cream *or* yogurt mixed with 2 tablespoons salsa, *or* to taste for dip

Put 1 teaspoon oil in a large sauté pan or wok, heat, and add cabbage, onion, garlic, celery, bell pepper, cumin, salt, and pepper. Toss and stir-fry on medium-high heat until vegetables begin to soften, about 5 minutes.

Add Tabasco sauce (if using), carrot, and lemon juice, toss, remove from heat, and drain in a strainer or colander. Try to remove as much liquid as possible. Put in a bowl, and stir in cilantro.

To wrap: Place a wrapper on flat surface, add about 2 heaping tablespoons of filling and fold like an envelope. Seal outer corner with a drop of water on fingertip. Once wrapped, the rolls should be cooked immediately.

To cook: In a large skillet (nonstick is fine), place 1 teaspoon of oil, heat, and add rolls. Cook on medium heat to brown each side. Remove to absorbent paper to drain, if necessary. Serve hot, cut in half, with a dip of sour cream or yogurt mixed with salsa, to taste.

SUMMER SALAD SANDWICH

SERVES 4 TO 6

Don't cook tonight, try vegetable sandwiches as an easy, creative, tasty, and light hot-weather meal. This colorful, low-cost, and healthy salad-on-bread, made with mostly raw vegetables, reminds me of one I had years ago at Cafe Fanny in Berkeley.

This versatile salad allows you to choose vegetables based on taste and seasonal availability. Look for fresh herbs at farmers' markets and the supermarket (or grow your own); dried herbs will also work. Mix with your favorite simple oil and vinegar dressing. Summer brings gobs of zucchini, onions, eggplant, and peppers to cook on the outdoor grill for yet another take on the sandwich. For more heft (in money and calories), add meat or cheese. Use a substantial country-style bread or try focaccia, the Italian flat bread easily found in most supermarkets. A thin baguette sliced lengthwise, filled, then cut into small pieces that are held together with toothpicks works well as an appetizer to serve with drinks.

1 bunch radishes, thinly sliced

1 medium red onion, thinly sliced

½ pound red potatoes, cooked, cooled, peeled, if desired, and thinly sliced

1 cucumber, peeled, seeded, and thinly sliced

3 ribs celery, thinly sliced

1 carrot, shaved into ribbons using a potato peeler

Small handful mixed fresh herbs such as thyme, oregano, basil, and parsley

Salt and pepper, to taste

¼ cup favorite simple oil and vinegar dressing, *or to* taste

3 tablespoons mayonnaise, olive paste (tapenade), *or* pesto, *or to* taste

8 to 10 slices favorite bread, *or* 1-pound loaf sliced lengthwise, a thin bread works best

In a bowl, mix the vegetables, herbs, salt, pepper, and dressing. Chill.

Spread bread with mayonnaise, tapenade, or pesto, and pile vegetables on top. Serve open-face if bread is thick, or covered if bread is thin.

EASY MORNING CAKE

MAKES 16 SQUARES

This not-too-sweet cake makes a nice addition for breakfast or brunch. If berries are used, they color the dough for a pretty and unusual presentation. Sour cream substitutes very easily for the yogurt. This cake doesn't need an electric beater and is easily mixed up in minutes. It's delicious for a brunch with eggs. Remember the texture is softer and spongier because there is little fat used.

Topping

¼ cup brown sugar

¼ cup granola *or* chopped walnuts *or* almonds

Cake

2 eggs

½ cup granulated sugar

¼ cup (½ stick) butter, melted and cooled

1 cup nonfat *or* lowfat plain yogurt *or* sour cream

1 teaspoon vanilla

¼ teaspoon lemon *or* almond extract

1½ teaspoons cinnamon

2 cups unbleached, all-purpose flour

½ teaspoon baking powder

1 teaspoon baking soda

¼ teaspoon salt

2 peaches, peeled and coarsely chopped, *or* use fruit of your choice, about 1 cup

Preheat oven to 350 degrees F.

Grease an 8 × 8-inch pan.

Make the topping. Mix brown sugar with granola or chopped nuts and set aside.

In a large bowl, beat eggs well with a fork. Add sugar and continue to beat. Add melted butter, yogurt, vanilla, lemon or almond extract, and cinnamon. Beat until well mixed.

Combine flour, baking powder, baking soda, and salt, and add to yogurt mixture. Add fruit and gently mix with fork just to incorporate. Mixture is thick.

Put mixture in prepared pan. Sprinkle with topping. Bake for 30 to 40 minutes or until top springs back to the touch and a toothpick comes out clean when pierced into the center. Serve warm or at room temperature with a dollop of ice cream, if desired.

TO CHEW ON

There is no love sincerer than the love of food.

—George Bernard Shaw

FAST PESTO DIP

MAKES 2 CUPS

I love this dip with fresh vegetables or pita bread. It takes seconds to make. Just add your favorite pesto—basil, sun-dried tomato, artichoke, to name a few—to lowfat or nonfat yogurt or sour cream. Prepared pestos are readily available—a little goes a long way even if the container seems expensive at the time. Or make your own with the recipe on page 148.

1 (16-ounce) container lowfat *or* nonfat yogurt *or* sour cream

2 tablespoons pesto, *or* to taste

Mix, taste for correct seasoning, refrigerate, and then serve.

QUICK CURRY DIP

MAKES 1 CUP

This quick dip is terrific with any vegetables. Try it with artichokes as a lowfat alternative to the usual butter or mayonnaise dip.

If curry isn't your thing, try a tablespoon or two of fresh basil or a prepared pesto dip. Or simply add a few teaspoons of Dijon mustard to the sour cream.

1 cup lowfat mayonnaise, nonfat sour cream, *or* nonfat yogurt *or* a mix
1 clove garlic, pressed
¼ teaspoon minced fresh ginger, *or* ½ teaspoon dried

Curry powder to taste, about ¼ to ½ teaspoon

Mix and taste for correct seasoning.

GARLIC DIP

MAKES ABOUT 1 CUP

Perfect as a last minute topping for salad, potatoes, or dip for fresh veggies.

1 cup plain nonfat yogurt *or* lowfat mayonnaise, *or* a mix

2 sprigs fresh parsley, finely chopped

1 small green onion, white plus a little green, finely chopped

1 small clove garlic, pressed

Dash Tabasco sauce, to taste, optional

Pinch salt, optional

Mix all ingredients and adjust for correct seasoning. Refrigerate until ready to serve.

PAN-FRIED ZUCCHINI WITH GARLIC AND CHEESE

SERVES 6

Simplicity makes this summer dish a winner. Zucchini and other thin-stemmed summer squash and fresh herbs abound in gardens or markets. Try this recipe with summer squashes of all varieties (the round shaped pattypan, for example). A sprinkling of Swiss or Parmesan cheese adds a little bite to the dish. Look for fresh basil or thyme in the produce section of the supermarket, at farmers' markets, or grow your own.

1 to 2 tablespoons olive oil or less
6 small-medium zucchini, about 1½ pounds, rinsed and cut into ½-inch rounds
4 medium-large garlic cloves, minced
2 teaspoons chopped fresh basil *or* thyme leaves
Salt and pepper, to taste
1 to 2 tablespoons freshly grated Swiss *or* Parmesan cheese

In a large nonstick skillet, heat oil to smoking point. Sauté half the zucchini for 5 minutes or until lightly golden brown, stirring and shaking the pan occasionally so squash won't stick. Transfer to a plate. Sauté the remainder of the zucchini.

Put all cooked zucchini back in the skillet and sprinkle with garlic, herbs, salt, and pepper. Lower the heat, cover the pan, and cook for about 5 minutes, turning 2 or 3 times. Uncover, sprinkle with cheese, cover again, cook over low heat for 2 minutes to just melt cheese. Serve immediately.

SARAH'S ZUCCHINI SAUCE

MAKES ABOUT 2 CUPS

Savvy Sarah, age six, has a thing about zucchini. She loves the taste and like many kids, is picky about how it looks when she eats this plentiful summer vegetable. Size, shape, and texture are important. Sarah's mom, Karen, began making this sauce when Sarah was just two. The sauce continues to be a hit with kids and grown-ups alike. Spinach can be substituted. Save time and steam zucchini in microwave oven.

1 small handful fresh basil leaves, parsley, or spinach, *or* a mix

1 small clove garlic, pressed

3 medium zucchini, chunked and steamed, reserve liquid

1 to 2 tablespoons olive oil

1 cup lowfat ricotta cheese

Salt and pepper, to taste

1 tablespoon grated Parmesan cheese, optional

1 pound cooked pasta

Put basil mixture and garlic into a blender or food processor and process until finely chopped. Add remaining ingredients except pasta and zucchini liquid and purée until smooth. Adjust seasoning and add reserved zucchini liquid if sauce is too thick.

Makes enough sauce for 1 pound of pasta. Toss with warm pasta and serve warm or at room temperature.

SUMMER STEW

SERVES 6

This is a rustic stew of summer's last crop of zucchini, toma-toes, and bell peppers. Corn from the cob and green beans make colorful additions. The flavoring comes from the sausage of your choice; any favorite well-spiced one will do.

Serve over rice or pasta, or solo with a salad and bread.

3 medium zucchini, cut into 1-inch chunks

3 medium onions, cut into eighths

3 small green bell peppers, coarsely chopped

3 medium potatoes, cut into 8 to 10 pieces

6 medium tomatoes, stemmed and coarsely chopped

1 cup water *or* broth

Salt and pepper, to taste

2 to 3 links Italian turkey sausage, *or* your fa-vorite, casing removed, and crumbled

2 tablespoons chopped fresh parsley

2 tablespoons grated Parme-san cheese

Put all ingredients, except sausage, parsley, and cheese, into a large pot.

Sprinkle sausage on top, cov-er, and cook on medium heat, mixing occasionally for 30 to 40 minutes or until vegeta-bles are cooked to desired softness.

Serve sprinkled with parsley and Parmesan cheese.

Appendix:
Basic Substitutions and Equivalents

BASIC SUBSTITUTIONS

Baking powder: 1 teaspoon = scant ½ teaspoon baking soda plus ½ teaspoon cream of tartar

Butter: 1 stick (¼ pound) = ½ cup or 8 tablespoons

Buttermilk or sour milk: 1 cup = 1 cup milk plus 1 tablespoon white vinegar or lemon juice left to curdle for 5 minutes

Buttermilk, nonfat yogurt, lowfat sour cream: Use interchangeably in many recipes

Cheese: (Cheddar, Jack, Swiss) 4 ounces = 1 cup shredded

Chocolate: 1 square (1 ounce) = 3 tablespoons unsweetened cocoa plus 1 tablespoon butter or oil

Eggs: 1 whole = 2 yolks for thickening

Flour: 2 tablespoons (for thickening) = 1 tablespoon cornstarch, rice or potato starch, or arrowroot

Flour: ⅞ cup all-purpose = 1 cup cake flour

Ginger: ½ teaspoon grated fresh = ¼ teaspoon ground ginger

Garlic: 1 clove = ⅛ teaspoon garlic powder

Honey: 1 cup = 1¼ cups sugar plus ¼ cup liquid

Lemon: 1 fresh = 2 to 3 tablespoons juice

Lemon: 1 fresh = about 2 teaspoons zest (grated peel); 1 teaspoon grated fresh peel = 1 teaspoon grated dry peel

Lemon juice: 1 teaspoon = ½ teaspoon vinegar

Milk: 1 cup = ½ cup evaporated milk plus ½ cup water

Milk: 1 cup = ⅓ cup nonfat dry milk plus 1 cup water

Milk: 1 cup = 1 cup fruit juice

Milk: 1 cup = 1 cup water plus 2 teaspoons butter

Onion: 1 medium = 2 teaspoons onion powder

Onion: ¼ cup diced = 1 tablespoon instant minced onion

Orange: 1 fresh = 6 to 8 tablespoons juice or 4 to 5 tablespoons reconstituted frozen juice

Orange: 1 teaspoon grated fresh peel = 1 teaspoon grated dry peel

Parsley: 2 tablespoons minced fresh = 1 tablespoon parsley flakes

Whipping cream: ½ pint (1 cup) = 2 cups whipped

MEASUREMENTS

3 teaspoons = 1 tablespoon

4 tablespoons = ¼ cup

16 tablespoons = 1 cup or 8 fluid ounces

2 cups = 16 fluid ounces or 1 pint

4 cups = 2 pints or 1 quart

1 liter = 1.06 quarts

4 quarts = 1 gallon

Herbs and Spices Chart

	American	Chinese	French	Indian	Italian	Mexican	Southeast Asian
Allspice	•		•			•	
Basil	•				•		•
Bay leaf*	•		•	•	•	•	
Black bean sauce		•					
Black beans, salted		•					
Capers	•		•		•		
Cayenne*	•						
Celery seed	•						
Chiles	•	•		•		•	•
Chives		•	•				•
Cilantro/coriander		•		•		•	•
Cinnamon*	•				•	•	
Cloves	•				•	•	
Coconut							•
Cumin*				•		•	•
Curry powder*				•			•
Dill*	•		•				
Fennel seed	•	•	•	•	•		
Fish sauce (nam pla)							•
Five spice powder		•					
Garam masala				•			
Garlic*	•	•	•	•	•	•	•
Ginger*		•		•			•
Hoisin sauce		•					
Lemon	•						•
Lemon grass							•
Lime	•			•		•	•

*Herbs and spices to always have on hand. This chart is a general guide. Feel free to create your own combinations.

	American	Chinese	French	Indian	Italian	Mexican	Southeast Asian
Mint	•			•	•	•	
Mustard or seed	•	•	•	•			
Nutmeg	•		•	•	•		
Orange zest	•	•	•		•		
Oregano*	•		•		•	•	
Paprika	•			•	•		
Parsley	•		•		•		
Rosemary*	•		•		•		
Sage	•				•		
Sesame oil		•					
Sesame seeds		•				•	
Soy		•					
Star anise		•					
Tamarind				•		•	•
Tarragon	•		•		•		
Thyme*	•		•		•		
Turmeric	•			•			•

Glossary of Terms and Techniques

Adjust seasoning: Same as "correct seasoning."

Bake: Cook covered or uncovered in dry heat, usually an oven.

Baste: Spoon or brush fat or liquid over cooking food to moisten and flavor.

Beat: Mix rapidly to include air and make smooth, using a spoon, fork, electric beater, or wire whisk.

Blanch: Same as "parboiling." Precook an ingredient (usually a vegetable or meat) in a pot of boiling water for a minute, more or less, depending on the size of the ingredient. Immediately drain and rinse under cold water to stop the cooking. Blanch to loosen skins of fruits and vegetables, leach salt and fat from meat, or precook vegetables ahead of time.

Blend: Combine well two or more ingredients, usually not with an electric mixer.

Boil: Heat liquid to make big rolling bubbles. Pasta cooks best in boiling water.

Braise: Brown ingredient with a little liquid, cover, and slowly cook.

Broil: Cook with direct high heat, usually in oven.

Chop: Cut in small pieces.

Correct seasoning: Taste food as it cooks and before serving to see that seasoning is to your taste. Also referred to as "adjust seasoning."

Dash: Small amount, few drops.

Done: When food can be removed from cooking heat. For meats and poultry, usually when pinkness disappears; for fish, when it barely flakes. Use your finger to press meat: It's rare if the meat is soft, and well-done if it's hard to the touch.

Fold: Gently combine a light ingredient with a heavier one, with up-and-down strokes, by hand rather than with a mixer.

Grease and flour: Prepare baking pan by lightly rubbing with butter or oil, then sprinkling with flour and shaking pan so flour clings. Tilt pan to dump excess flour.

Grill: Cook over direct heat, as on a barbecue.

Mince: Chop very fine.

Pan fry: Cook foods in an open skillet on the stove.

Poach: Gently cook in simmering liquid.

Press: Squeeze a clove of garlic in a small gadget (a garlic press) that squashes it to pulp.

Purée: Mash until smooth.

Simmer: Heat liquid so it makes few, if any, bubbles for gentle or long cooking.

Skim: Remove fat from liquid with a spoon.

Steam: Cook in a basket or on a rack suspended above boiling water or liquid.

Stir-fry: Cook bite-size pieces of food in a skillet or wok on high heat. Food is constantly tossed so it cooks quickly and evenly.

Taste: Try food as it cooks so seasoning can be adjusted to preference.

Zest: Thin outer peel of citrus fruit, not including white inner layer. Use a fine grater, a gadget called a zester, or a vegetable peeler to shear the outer layer, then finely mince.

Selected References

Aidells, Bruce and Denis Kelly. *Real Beer and Good Eats.* New York: Alfred A. Knopf, 1993.

Beard, James and Sam Aaron. *How to Eat Better for Less Money.* Second revised edition. New York: Simon and Schuster, 1970.

Corn, Elaine. *Gooey Desserts.* Rocklin, CA: Prima Publishing, 1994.

Culinary Institute of America. *Cooking Secrets of the CIA.* San Francisco: Chronicle Books, 1995.

Food Marketing Institute, "Trends in the United States: Consumer Attitudes and the Supermarket, 1996." Washington, 1996.

Food Marketing Institute and *Prevention Magazine*, "Shopping for Health Report." Washington, 1996.

Friedland, Susan. *The Passover Table.* New York: HarperPerennial, 1994.

Goldstein, Joyce. *Mediterranean: the Beautiful Cookbook.* San Francisco: HarperCollins Publishers, 1994.

Heatter, Maida. *Maida Heatter's Brand-New Book of Great Cookies.* New York: Random House, 1995.

Klivans, Elinor. *Bake and Freeze Desserts:* 130 Do-Ahead Cakes, Pies, Cookies, Brownies, Bars, Ice Creams, Terrines, and Sorbets. *New York:* William Morrow and Company, Inc., 1994.

Lalli, Carole. *Chicken Salads.* New York: HarperCollins, 1994.

Margen, Sheldon, M.D., and The Editors of the University of California at Berkeley Wellness Letter. *The Wellness Encyclopedia of Food and Nutrition.* New York: Rebus, 1992.

Nathan, Joan. *The Jewish Holiday Kitchen.* New York: Schocken Books, 1988.

Neal, Bill. *Bill Neal's Southern Cooking, Revised.* Chappel Hill: The University of North Carolina Press, 1989.

Ornish, Dean. *Eat More, Weigh Less.* New York: HarperCollins, 1993.

Robbins, Tom. *Jitterbug Perfume.* New York: Bantam, 1984.

Rombauer, Irma and Marion Rombauer Becker, *Joy of Cooking.* New York: New American Library, 1973.

Shaw, David. *The Pleasure Police: How Bluenose Busybodies and Lily-Livered Alarmists are Taking All the Fun Out of Life.* New York: Doubleday, 1996.

Taylor, John Martin. *Hoppin' John's Lowcountry Cooking.* New York: Bantam, 1992.

United States Department of Agriculture. *The Food Pyramid Guide.* 1992.

United States Department of Agriculture. Economic Research Service. "Food Prices to Post Moderate Gains in 1996." Clauson, Annette. *Agricultural Outlook,* July, 1996.

Weaver, William Woys. *The Christmas Cook: Three Centuries of American Yuletide Sweets.* New York: HarperPerennial, 1990.

Index

International Conversion Chart

These are not exact equivalents: they've been slightly rounded to make measuring easier.

Liquid Measurements

American	Imperial	Metric	Australian
2 tablespoons (1 oz.)	1 fl. oz.	30 ml	1 tablespoon
¼ cup (2 oz.)	2 fl. oz.	60 ml	2 tablespoons
⅓ cup (3 oz.)	3 fl. oz.	80 ml	¼ cup
½ cup (4 oz.)	4 fl. oz.	125 ml	⅓ cup
⅔ cup (5 oz.)	5 fl. oz.	165 ml	½ cup
¾ cup (6 oz.)	6 fl. oz.	185 ml	⅔ cup
1 cup (8 oz.)	8 fl. oz.	250 ml	¾ cup

Spoon Measurements

American	Metric
¼ teaspoon	1 ml
½ teaspoon	2 ml
1 teaspoon	5 ml
1 tablepoon	15 ml

Oven Temperatures

Fahrenheit	Centigrade	Gas
250	120	½
300	150	2
325	160	3
350	180	4
375	190	5
400	200	6
450	230	8

Weights

US/UK	Metric
1 oz.	30 grams (g)
2 oz.	60 g
4 oz. (¼ lb)	125 g
5 oz. (⅓ lb)	155 g
6 oz.	185 g
7 oz.	220 g
8 oz. (½ lb)	250 g
10 oz.	315 g
12 oz. (¾ lb)	375 g
14 oz.	440 g
16 oz. (1 lb)	500 g
2 lbs.	1 kg